WOMEN
OF THE
WHITE
HOUSE

Published in 2021 by Welbeck

An Imprint of Welbeck Non-Fiction Limited, part of Welbeck Publishing Group.
Based in London and Sydney.
www.welbeckpublishing.com

A CIP catalogue record for this book is available from the British Library

ISBN 978 1 78739 388 2

Printed in Dongguan, China

10 9 8 7 6 5 4 3 2

MIX
Paper from
responsible sources
FSC® C144853

★

WOMEN
OF THE
WHITE
HOUSE

THE ILLUSTRATED STORY OF THE FIRST LADIES
OF THE UNITED STATES OF AMERICA

AMY RUSSO

AFTERWORD BY
ANTHONY J EKSTEROWICZ

WELBECK

CONTENTS

INTRODUCTION

BY AMY RUSSO

AFTER MORE THAN 200 YEARS OF AMERICAN PRESIDENTIAL ELECTIONS, ATTAINING THE WEST WING IS ONE GLASS CEILING WOMEN HAVE YET TO BREAK.

Through the East Wing, the office of the First Lady, they've come close. First ladies haven't always wielded major influence. Some, such as Martha Washington and Pat Nixon, came to the job reluctantly, even lamenting their husband's elections. Others, like Eleanor Roosevelt and Hillary Clinton, carefully cultivated power, acting not only as presidential allies, but politicians in their own right, their clout outlasting their time in the White House.

Certain first ladies made their mark more quietly. Abigail Adams regularly exchanged letters with her husband, famously urging him to "Remember the Ladies, and be more generous and favourable to them than your ancestors" as the Founding Fathers prepared to write what would become the Declaration of Independence.[1]

Sarah Polk, despite turning a cold shoulder to the suffragist movement, was perhaps equally adept in seeking influence for herself. Aware that the nation's capitol was a male-dominated sphere, she recast her positions as those of her husband's by prefacing her own thoughts with "Mr. Polk believes."[2]

Like the many women who've borne the title of first lady, the role itself has transformed with time. At its inception in the eighteenth century, expectations were heavily centred on hostessing, from arranging social events to overseeing renovations and preparing the White House for guests. To those who were strategic, even teatime provided a pathway to power.

Take, for example, Louisa Adams. Before becoming first lady, she established a tradition of weekly tea parties. The most crucial of all may have taken place in 1825, when her husband, then-Secretary of State John Quincy Adams, was locked in a battle for the presidency against Andrew Jackson, who had just won the popular vote as well as a plurality of electoral votes. To win, John Quincy needed the backing of the House of Representatives.

According to his diary, 67 representatives attended Louisa's soirée, which took place the night before their decision.[3] The next day, John Quincy was elected president.

Dolley Madison was another hostessing maven who put her skills to political use, organizing her so-called weekly squeezes during which politicians from both sides of the aisle packed into the White House. Her interpersonal ingenuity made her a liaison for the president in one distinct instance as conflict brewed with the British. Knowing her husband couldn't align himself with war hawk House speaker Henry Clay, she bonded with the speaker herself by dipping snuff with him.[4]

At times, when presidents have been in need most, first ladies have been their confidantes and protectors. The closest any has come to the presidency, arguably, was Edith Wilson, who after Woodrow Wilson's stroke in 1919, acted as guardian and gatekeeper. She later wrote in her memoir that she "studied every paper, sent from the different Secretaries or Senators, and tried to digest and present in tabloid form the things that, despite my vigilance, had to go to the President."[5]

While women have yet to be elected to the presidency, they've no doubt been made, by choice and by circumstance, integral to the fabric of the White House.

First ladies, unlike presidents, ultimately serve by circumstance in a role that's been defined by culture rather than the Constitution. There is no job description and there are no codified rules. In that, there is agency. Those who have come to shape the legacy of the East Wing the most have embraced its capacity for influence with political acumen, passion and the ability to act as allies and agents of change.

MARTHA DANDRIDGE CUSTIS WASHINGTON

(1731–1802)

She was "Lady Washington," "The Presidentess," or to her loved ones, "Patsy," but Martha Washington would become known to history as the *first* first lady – the woman who defined the role of the president's wife as the nation was still coming to terms with its newfound independence.

Born in 1731 on her family's Chestnut Grove plantation New Kent County, Virginia, Martha was the eldest of eight children. When she was just 17 years old, wealthy landowner Daniel Parke Custis became smitten with Martha, though he was 20 years her senior. His father, John Custis IV, was a notoriously curmudgeonly man, so unhappily married that his own tombstone states his life existed solely within the mere seven years he spent in his Arlington bachelor's home.[1] It was in large part due to that surly disposition that his son had remained unmarried for so long.[2] When Daniel announced he wanted to ask for Martha's hand, John balked at the idea, claiming her family's financial status wasn't up to par.[3]

Finally, John was persuaded to meet Martha in the company of James Power, a lawyer.[4] Historians aren't sure exactly what was said, though according to a message from James to Daniel, John "heartily and willingly" gave his blessing, declaring there was no other woman in Virginia more fit to marry his son.[5] Combined with her quiet strength, Martha's warmth and charm would become her trademark traits, as well as a guiding philosophy throughout a life destined for hardship.

Martha outlived each of her four children and her husband, who died suddenly in 1757, just seven years into their marriage. Incidentally, she was left with a 17,500-acre plantation and nearly 300 slaves, making her incredibly wealthy at the age of 26.[6]

While married women at the time, under British common law, could not own property, but unmarried women had more rights. Daniel's death gave Martha newfound power, placing her in a managerial role in which she oversaw his estate as a widow.

Though she was mourning the loss of her husband, Martha met George Washington the following year, in 1758. However, with no financial need to marry, their partnership would need to be built on love. George, then a distinguished colonel in the Virginia Regiment, was known to have enjoyed the company of women, but with Martha, he was smitten.[7] By 1759, the two had tied the knot.

Within months, the newlyweds moved to Mount Vernon, a massive estate on which George's father, Augustine, had built a mansion in 1734. The couple arrived with several slaves and Martha's children, four-year-old Jacky and two-year-old Patsy, in tow. Her other two children, Daniel and Frances, had already died under the age of five.

The sprawling property served as Martha's training ground for the White House, as she planned dinners, hosted guests, and oversaw textile-making and the sewing of clothing for the estate's slaves.[8]

Though these were Martha's so-called "golden years," they were punctuated by her daughter's chronic struggle with epilepsy.[9] She died at age 17 in 1773 following a seizure.

In 1775, the start of the American Revolutionary War pulled the Washingtons away from the comforts of Mount Vernon and to the frontlines of battle for eight years. Assuming an active role in the war effort, Martha spent almost half of that period with George, now a general leading the Continental Army, who felt her presence so crucial that he asked Congress to foot the bill for her travel.[10]

At Valley Forge, where a brutal winter and dwindling morale signaled a low point in the war, Martha turned to her role as a hostess to renew the troops' spirits with luxurious dinners. Aside from entertaining, as historian Patricia Brady, author of *Martha Washington: An American Life*, noted, her role could be understood partly by the shift in her sewing habits.[11] While women of means would work on tapestry and embroidery, Martha broke out her knitting needles and made socks for infantrymen who marched until they wore through.[12] She also

raised funds to create linen shirts for the soldiers' uniforms.

Having already lost three of her children, Martha again faced hardship when Jacky, who had enlisted in the war, died in Yorktown in 1781. It is believed that he contracted typhus.

In 1783, the war came to its official end, and the Washingtons retired to Mount Vernon once again, where they spent six years before George was elected president in 1789. The change uprooted Martha from the estate, a stinging sacrifice for the now first lady. In a letter to niece Fanny, written months after the election when Martha was living in New York, the nation's temporary capital, Martha revealed that

ABOVE: Martha and George Washington pictured with the first lady's grandchildren through marriage: Eleanor Parke Custis Lewis (left) and George Washington Parke Custis (right).

her life seemed "dull" and that she felt "more like a state prisoner than anything else," adding that there were "certain bounds set for me which I must not depart from."[13]

In another letter to Massachusetts playwright and chronicler Mercy Otis Warren, Martha said she had expected that she and George would be "left to grow old in solitude and tranquility together" at Mount Vernon, calling the change of course a disappointment.[14] Nonetheless, when called to the White House, she rose to the occasion.

Martha's 11-day trip to New York was marked by great fanfare, fireworks, and 13-gun salutes.[15] To this day, she remains the first and only woman to be featured as the primary portrait on U.S. currency, a sign of her iconic status in the new government.

As first lady, Martha hosted formal dinners each Thursday and public receptions each Friday at the presidential residence, opening the doors to anyone of good social standing who wished to attend. Visitors ranged from members of Congress and dignitaries to local community members.[16] However, the events were met with criticism from sceptics who felt Martha was imitating the British monarchy from whose grip America had just escaped.[17] Conversely, Abigail Adams, the wife of then-Vice President John Adams, praised Martha's poise, calling her "the object of veneration and Respect."[18] Like the first lady herself, the nation was still shaping its identity and defining its new position in the world. There was no how-to manual and each of Martha's actions had the power to set a precedent for her successors.

In 1791, the capital was relocated to Philadelphia, and Martha had gradually adjusted to her new position, finding more friends there than she had in New York.[20] Still, she missed life at Mount Vernon, a longing which only grew during her husband's tumultuous second term, during which he struggled to hold together the new nation despite emerging partisanship, tension within his cabinet, and foreign wars.

His decision against serving a third term came as a relief to Martha, who made her final return to Mount Vernon with George in 1797.

Two years later, George died after contracting a throat infection, leaving Martha a widow once more.[21] While she mourned, the nation mourned with her. Thousands of citizens sent her condolence letters, and many asked for momentos.[22] Shortly after, Martha, who one visitor recalled had begun speaking of "death as a pleasant journey,"[23] died in 1802 of a severe fever, and was buried alongside George on the estate where she had once longed to retire.[24]

BEING ON THE DOLLAR BILL

Martha Washington remains the first and only woman to be featured as the primary portrait on U.S. currency, a sign of her iconic status in the new government.

Design on the one-dollar bill began in the summer of 1886. The bill was a Silver Certificate and could be redeemed for one silver dollar coin. These bills were produced six years after George Washington was first featured on a bill – a slightly re-designed Martha Washington also was produced in 1891 and the $1 Certificates were discontinued in 1957. Several newspapers featured quotes from prominent individuals upon the issuance of the Martha Washington Silver Certificate: "Persons fortunate enough to possess a one-dollar Silver Certificate have an excellent picture of Martha Washington, the wife of the Father of His Country," said the *Indiana Democrat* in 1901.[25]

ABIGAIL
SMITH ADAMS

(1744–1818)

Confidante, advisor, and "dearest friend" to husband John Adams, Abigail Adams's role as first lady was undoubtedly shaped by her bond with the president. In fact, much of the influence she exhibited in the role was demonstrated long before the couple entered the White House.

Born in Weymouth, Massachusetts, in on 11 November 1744 to distinguished parents William Smith, a Congregationalist minister, and Elizabeth Quincy, a descendant of the politically active Quincy family, Abigail immediately entered a life of privilege. As was the case for many women at the time, she was not formally educated. However, Abigail learned at home to read and write, and spent much of her time either with her nose in a book or corresponding with loved ones.[1] Her early love of writing would become a cornerstone of her relationship with John, at the same time providing historians with an extensive and invaluable record of her thoughts on her transition to power.

In 1764, at the age of 19, she married the would-be president, who was embarking on a law career. She become a mother almost instantly, giving birth to the first of her six children nearly nine months into their marriage. While John's work both as a lawyer and a political revolutionary caused him to travel, Abigail held down the fort at home, managing their property and business affairs all while caring for her children.[2] Though British property laws stipulated that married women couldn't own property, Abigail began referring to their land as her own, even taking on investment decisions.[3]

In 1774, John went to Philadelphia as a delegate to the First Continental Congress, a trip that resulted in a prolonged separation between the two. The distance prompted the couple to begin writing letters to each other, which would become a lifelong tradition and a hallmark of their enduring love.

Of the 1,160 missives that have survived, the most famous was written by Abigail to John in 1776 as he served in the Second Continental Congress, which was drafting the Declaration of Independence. Knowing her husband had a hand in defining the laws of the new nation, Abigail urged him to "Remember the Ladies, and be more generous and favourable to them than your ancestors."[4]

Continuing, she warned that John's failure to heed her advice could result in grave consequences. "Do not put such unlimited power into the hands of the Husbands," she wrote. "Remember all men would be tyrants if they could. If perticular [sic] care and attention is not pail to the ladies, we are determined to foment a Rebellion, and will not hold ourselves bound by any Laws in which we have no voice, or Representation."

In that same letter, Abigail also voiced her opposition to slavery. "I have sometimes been ready to think that the passion for Liberty cannot be Equally Strong in the Breasts of those who have been accustomed to deprive their fellow Creatures of theirs," she wrote, calling enslavement antithetical to the Christian "principal of doing to others as we would that others should do unto us."

Though the abolition of slavery wouldn't be seen for nearly 90 years and women's suffrage wouldn't arrive for another 55, Abigail's letter was an early act of advocacy for slaves as well as a push for female representation in government.

Perhaps ironically, as was the case with Martha Washington, when it came to the role of first lady Abigail recoiled at the prospect, dreading the position months before her husband's 1797 inauguration. In a particularly colourful letter penned in the winter of 1796, she told John that she had envisioned retiring at their Peacefield farm property rather than becoming first lady, a job she said was akin to being "fastened up Hand and foot and Tongue to be shot at as our Quincy Lads do at the poor Geese and Turkies."[5]

In a subsequent letter to John as his inauguration loomed, Adams's concerns didn't wane. "My pen runs riot," she wrote, noting that while she "must grow cautious and prudent," she fretted life would become "a dull business when such restrictions are laid upon it."[6]

Months after her husband assumed the presidency, Abigail wrote to her sister, Mary Smith Cranch, that she "expected to be vilified and abused" in the new position.[7] When it came to her assessments of politicians she perceived to be the president's foes, Abigail indeed sparked backlash from detractors including Republican Albert Gallatin, who declared, "She is Mrs. President not of the United States but of a faction.... It is not right."[?]

Albeit Abigail's transition to public life was a challenge, John developed a deep respect for his wife's insights, telling her after his election, "I never wanted your Advice and assistance more in my life."[8] Abigail soon became an outspoken ally of the president, often backing his positions, which included championing the 1798 Alien and Sedition Acts, a controversial set of laws stripping immigrants of political power, making deportations easier, and muzzling the press.[9]

When it came to media attention, Abigail only further showed herself to be a fierce defender of her husband's image. According to the University of Virginia's Miller Center, on occasion the first lady went so far as to plant "stories in Boston's newspapers, discreetly sending home letters and articles she hoped to have published."[10]

Though the extent of Abigail's influence on

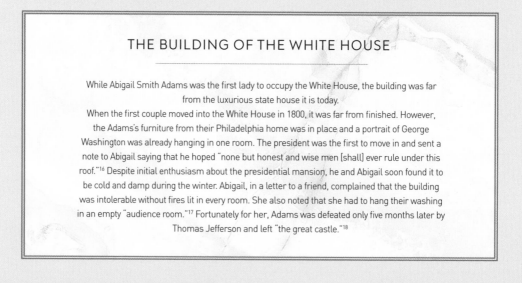

THE BUILDING OF THE WHITE HOUSE

While Abigail Smith Adams was the first lady to occupy the White House, the building was far from the luxurious state house it is today.

When the first couple moved into the White House in 1800, it was far from finished. However, the Adams's furniture from their Philadelphia home was in place and a portrait of George Washington was already hanging in one room. The president was the first to move in and sent a note to Abigail saying that he hoped "none but honest and wise men [shall] ever rule under this roof."[16] Despite initial enthusiasm about the presidential mansion, he and Abigail soon found it to be cold and damp during the winter. Abigail, in a letter to a friend, complained that the building was intolerable without fires lit in every room. She also noted that she had to hang their washing in an empty "audience room."[17] Fortunately for her, Adams was defeated only five months later by Thomas Jefferson and left "the great castle."[18]

ABOVE A watercolor painting of Abigail Adams Smith House from 1917 in Manhattan's Upper East Side.

her husband is debatable, critics took note of her standing, mocking her as "Mrs. President."[11] While he valued her counsel, when it came to politics, the two didn't always see eye to eye. For instance, during the XYZ Affair, a diplomatic conflict between the U.S. and France, Abigail advocated for war with France, though John pushed for a peaceful solution.[12]

By 1800, Abigail and the president had moved into the White House, becoming the first to reside at 1600 Pennsylvania Avenue in the new capital of Washington, D.C. Aside from consulting with her husband, like the first lady before her and the others to come, Abigail took up the role of hostess, receiving visitors at public ceremonies and weekly dinners attended by lawmakers, diplomats, and prominent citizens.[13]

Despite her initial reservations about becoming first lady, when her husband's tenure came to a close, Abigail felt it was a personal loss, writing; "I can truly and from my heart say that the most mortifying circumstance attendant upon my retirement from public life is, that my power of doing good to my fellow creatures is curtailed and diminished, but tho' the means is wanting, the will and the wish remain."[14]

As author John B. Roberts states in his 2004 book, *Rating The First Ladies*, Abigail's statement "reveals the modern nature of this unusual woman," who, unlike her predecessor, defined her role in part on the wish to be "an equal voice in shaping the new nation's affairs."[15]

MARTHA WAYLES SKELTON JEFFERSON

(1748 – 82)

While Martha Washington was the *first* first lady and Abigail Adams was the first to live in the White House, Martha Jefferson would become known as the first of the presidents' wives to die before seeing her husband's election.

Already a widow when she met Thomas Jefferson, Martha was 22-years-old when he began his courtship. She had just one son from her first marriage to plantation owner Bathurst Skelton, who died in 1768, two years after their wedding. Faced with tremendous loss at a young age, she then lost her son, who died three years later.

Amid the hardships, Martha found a companion in Thomas, whom she married the following year in 1772. She brought with her a hefty inheritance from her father's death that year, which gave her slaves and roughly 11,000 acres of land.[1] As a married woman, by law, the property became her husband's, meaning Thomas's wealth was an acquired benefit of his union with Martha.

During the first years of their marriage, Thomas was a member of the House of Burgesses, and later served in the Second Continental Congress where he helped to draft the Declaration of Independence. In 1779, he began his term as Governor of Virginia as the Revolutionary War waged on.

At that time, Martha was called on by Martha Washington to spearhead an effort by women in the state to support militiamen by fundraising and gathering supplies. Though the role held great significance, her diminishing health prevented her from actively participating, requiring a substitute to take her place.

Unlike the extensive collection of letters preserved from Abigail and John Adams's relationship, a mere four documents in Martha's handwriting are known to have survived, leaving certain details of her life a mystery.[2] It is for that reason that much of the information that exists about Martha has been relayed through second-hand sources.

As explained by Emilie Johnson, an assistant curator at Monticello, the Jeffersons' Charlottesville estate, Martha remains "for many people, kind of a question mark," partly because Thomas "burned their correspondence in an effort to keep their relationship private."[3]

In a particularly poignant note penned weeks or days before her death in September 1782, Martha copied several lines from Laurence Sterne's novel, *Tristram Shandy*:[4]

> *Time wastes too fast: every letter*
> *I trace tells me with what rapidity*
> *life follows my pen. The days and hours*
> *of it are flying over our heads like*
> *clouds of windy day never to return –*
> *more. Every thing presses on –*

Thomas later completed the quote himself:

> *and every time I kiss thy hand to bid*
> *adieu, every absence which follows it, are*
> *preludes to that eternal separation which*
> *we are shortly to make!*

30 OCTOBER 1748 // Born in Charles City, Virginia, to John Wyles, an attorney and businessman, and Martha Eppes

1766 // Marries Bathurst Skelton

7 NOVEMBER 1767 // Their son, John, is born

30 SEPTEMBER 1768 // Skelton dies suddenly

1771 // John dies of a fever

1772 // Martha marries Thomas Jefferson

1779 // Thomas Jefferson becomes Governor of Virginia, with Martha becoming first lady of Virginia

3 JUNE 1781 // Martha dies due to health complications linked to successive pregnancies

1801 // Thomas Jefferson assumes the presidency, but never remarries

Historians are not certain of the cause of Martha's death, but a letter from Thomas to French officer Marquis de Chastellux appears to indicate she became ill after bearing the last of her seven children.[5] In the message, Thomas laments "the state of dreadful suspense in which I had been kept all the summer and the catastrophe which closed it."[6] According to the White House Historical Association, the physical toll of frequent pregnancies had weakened Martha so severely that Thomas pulled back on his political life to be by her side.[7]

ABOVE A gold watch key once owned by Thomas Jefferson. The timepiece is engraved with Martha Jefferson's name, birth date and the date of her death, and contains a braided lock of her hair.

In his note to de Chastellux, it is clear her death devastated Thomas, who said it "wiped away all my plans and left me a blank which I had not the spirits to fill up."[8]

Decades later, Thomas's granddaughter, Ellen Wayles Randolph Coolidge, recalled it in a letter as "the bitterest grief my grandfather ever knew," noting that "no second wife was ever called to take her place."[9]

While it proved an emotional strain to Thomas, it was that same loss that seems to have pushed him to dive further into his political career as he became the newly formed government's ambassador to France in 1784, taking with him eldest daughter Martha "Patsy" Jefferson Randolph. This can also be gleaned from his correspondence with de Chastellux, in which he writes that it was "in this state of mind" following the death that he accepted the post.[10]

In 1801, having been a widower for 19 years,

ABOVE One of very few examples of correspondence between Martha and Thomas Jefferson that survive to this day.

Thomas assumed the presidency, and Patsy periodically took her mother's place as the White House hostess, albeit only for two seasons, the winters of 1802 and 1806.[11] At the same time, as Andrew Burstein, author of *The Inner Jefferson*, states, Patsy ran Monticello, placing her in charge of her father's massive plantation.[12] Dolley Madison, future first lady and wife of the next president, James Madison, also stepped in at times to lend a hand with White House events.

Though Martha did not live to play the role of first lady, it may have been in the mourning of her loss that Thomas was propelled to continue the political career that led him to the presidency.

DOLLEY PAYNE TODD MADISON

(1768–1849)

FIRST LADY: 4 MARCH 1809–4 MARCH 1817

The role of first lady was still being shaped by each woman who filled it – Martha Washington brought her charm as a hostess and Abigail Adams brought an outspoken voice eager to influence politics. If there was ever a woman who knew how to combine the two, it was Dolley Madison.

Born in 1768 to a well-heeled Virginian family in Guilford County, North Carolina, Dolley, one of eight children, moved to Philadelphia at age 15. Seven years later, she abided by her father's dying wish for her to marry a Quaker lawyer, John Todd, with whom she had two children.[1] By then, it appeared Dolley was destined for a comfortable life of domesticity, but when the yellow fever epidemic hit the city in 1793, her world was shaken. Dolley lost her newborn baby, her husband and her in-laws to the disease, leaving her single with an 18-month-old son. As a widow, she came into ownership of her husband's property, and was, in that respect, both empowered and free, but it wouldn't be long before her next marriage.[2]

Dolley had become close with Aaron Burr, the future vice president infamously accused of treason, who, as a favour to James Madison, introduced the two.[3] Mere months after having met, James and Dolley tied the knot in 1794. James already wielded substantial political power as one of the Founding Fathers and a member of the House of Representatives, and soon, Dolley too would find her own place in that world.

The newlyweds lived in James's Montpelier plantation house in Orange County, Virginia, for a short time, before moving to Washington, D.C. in 1801 when he was named Secretary of State by then-President Thomas Jefferson. As the president had been widowed for almost two decades, Dolley occasionally filled in as the White House hostess. However, her F Street residence became, for the Madisons, an even more vibrant social hub where entertaining blended with politics, enhancing the power of Dolley's role.[4]

As observed by Margaret Bayard Smith, a contemporary Washington political commentator, the home "was the resort of most company," surpassed only by the White House.[5] Among the movers and shakers were an array of diplomats and politicians.[6]

Becoming further enmeshed in government affairs, Dolley herself became a political symbol in 1803 during what became known as the "Merry Affair."[7] That year, the British had sent Anthony Merry, their first foreign minister, and his wife to the White House for dinner with President Jefferson. In a defiant breach of etiquette intended as a silent pro-democracy protest, Thomas escorted Dolley into the dining room rather than the diplomat's wife.[8] The president subsequently established the "pêle-mêle" rule stipulating "that no man here would come to dinner where he was to be marked with inferiority to any other."[9]

In 1808, following her husband's election as president, Dolley made the complete transition into her role as first lady. Upon moving into the White House, she redesigned its gathering spaces

with the help of British architect Benjamin Latrobe, opting for neoclassical decor.[10] The decision wasn't just fashionable: it was political, meant to signify a commitment to the civic virtues embodied by traditional republicanism.[11] The rooms were then used for weekly "squeezes," bipartisan receptions that earned the name because of the overwhelming number of politicians jam-packed into the house.[12]

Aside from arranging social events, Dolley also acted as a political liaison for her husband. As conflict brewed with the British, she knew the president could not align himself with War Hawk Speaker of the House, Henry Clay, so she made an ally of the speaker by dipping snuff with him.[13] As one of her friends later said, the snuff box "has a magic influence."[14]

By the end of her husband's second presidential term in 1816, Dolley had spent 15 years in the capital, and would return to Montpelier for the remainder of James's life. In 1836, she was widowed, and moved back to Washington seven years later. For Dolley, it was a homecoming. She spent the last of her years living across from the White House on Lafayette Square, hosting crowded receptions just as she had done during her time as first lady.

According to a newspaper announcement of her funeral in 1849, the ceremony was attended by an array of Washington's elite – from the president

and his cabinet to diplomats, congressmen, and supreme court judges – serving as a testament to Dolley's reputation and the respect she commanded in her time.[15]

OPPOSITE An engraving of the first lady clutching a document for safekeeping, which she is pictured rescuing as British troops invaded Washington and set fire to the White House in 1814.

ABOVE A portrait of Dolley Madison c. 1817.

INTO THE FLAMES

Though examples of the first lady's political victories are many, Dolley Madison is perhaps best remembered for her tenacious bravery during the War of 1812 when British troops set fire to the White House. As evacuations ensued, Dolley instructed 15-year-old Paul Jennings, an enslaved African-American, to remove Gilbert Stuart's portrait of George Washington from the wall.[16] If that was not possible, she demanded it be destroyed so that it not be taken by the British as a trophy.[17] As time ran short, Dolley eventually ordered Paul to smash the frame and cut the canvas out with a knife.[18] According to a letter written by Dolley to sister Lucy Todd, purportedly from within the burning house, she had insisted on remaining inside until the portrait was rescued.[19] The letter was then given to Bayard Smith, who published it in 1836. Facing scepticism for allegedly inflating the account to boost her image,[20] Dolley defended her story years later, writing, "not that I felt a desire to gain laurels – but should there be a merit in remaining an hour in danger of life or liberty to save the likeness of anything, the merit in this case belongs to me."[21]

ELIZABETH KORTRIGHT MONROE

(1768 – 1830)

FIRST LADY: 4 MARCH 1817–4 MARCH 1825

Unlike certain of her predecessors, Elizabeth Monroe took a remarkably reticent approach to her role as first lady, and would be remembered for her embrace of formality and old-world European customs: a stark contrast to the attitudes of the still newly independent nation.

Little is known about the details of Elizabeth's childhood, personal life, and views as nearly no documents in her writing remain in existence today. Born in 1768 to a wealthy family in New York City, she met James Monroe at age 16, marrying him the following year.[1] According to Daniel Preston, an editor for the Papers of James Monroe Project at the University of Mary Washington, the two "were absolutely devoted."[2]

In 1794, Elizabeth began taking some involvement in her husband's political life, traveling with him to France after President George Washington appointed him minister to the country. Together, the Monroes were tasked with promoting a serious image of the U.S. as a world power while avoiding causing any offence to the French government.[3] Elizabeth adapted seamlessly, learning the language, the etiquette and the culture, an effort so thorough she was nicknamed "La Belle Americainne." Elizabeth didn't just blossom in France – she thrived.

During the French Revolution, Elizabeth made a perhaps uncharacteristically bold effort to rescue from prison Adrienne de Noailles de Lafayette, the wife of Marquis de Lafayette, a friend of the president as well as a major general who fought alongside the Continental Army for American independence.[4] After Elizabeth visited her in prison, the French government set Noailles free, concerned over straining relations with its U.S. ally.[5]

In 1799, following the Monroes' return to the States, James was elected governor of Virginia. Throughout his four-year term, Elizabeth's health fell into a serious decline, which historians suspect was triggered by epilepsy, an illness about which little was known at the time. For the first-lady-to-be, this meant withdrawal from social functions and public interaction.

Her reclusive nature was especially evident during James's time as Secretary of State from 1811 to 1817, during which time Elizabeth was mostly seen at official events and neglected to return social calls.[6] Even during James's presidential inauguration in 1817, Elizabeth made herself scarce and was absent for his swearing-in ceremony.[7]

It is believed that James burned all but one of her letters after her death, leaving behind virtually no correspondence between the two to shed light on her role during his presidency. However, in the way of politics, her influence seems to have been minimal.

Her focus was primarily aimed at optics and appearances – both her own and that of White House events. She had brought with her from Europe a deep appreciation for the Continent's customs, speaking French with her family and having White House dinners served "English style," pairing one servant with each guest.[8]

As Elizabeth's role became complicated by her fragile health and she became further distant from her duties, the couple's daughter Eliza often stepped in as White House hostess.

It was likely a challenge for Elizabeth to fill Dolley Madison's shoes, as much of history remarks upon the contrast between the two. As Preston states, Elizabeth "did not like large crowds," and found it "very uncomfortable at the large receptions that the president had," despite being social among smaller groups.[9] It was a sharp departure from the days

ABOVE: A portrait of Elizabeth Monroe's daughter, Eliza Monroe Hay, who frequently filled in as hostess while the first lady's health declined.

when Dolley would entertain hordes of politicians and diplomats at her weekly receptions.

While not much evidence exists of Elizabeth's political role in Washington, her formal social customs would be followed by her successors and leave a mark on White House culture that lasted years.[10]

ABOVE: Oak Hill, a property James Monroe inherited from his uncle in 1808. A mansion was subsequently constructed on the grounds, and the Monroes used it as a second home.

EUROPEAN STYLE

As presidential scholar Richard Norton Smith notes, Elizabeth was accused of harbouring an "obsession with fashion," and is believed to have paid as much as $1,500 for one of her gowns.[11] Controversy brewed over her love of European style, a reflection of a monarchical past which a newly formed nation of democratic values had rejected. Elizabeth was fond of costume jewellery featuring large crucifixes, accessories beloved by the elite Catholic classes of France and Spain, but unusual for a Protestant American lady.

The president himself provoked backlash with his purchases of French-made furniture, prompting Congress to enact legislation stating that only American-made furniture should be bought for the White House.[12] Though James took control of the furnishings, it is likely that Elizabeth would have influenced his decisions on such matters.[13]

LOUISA CATHERINE JOHNSON ADAMS

(1775–1852)

FIRST LADY: 4 MARCH 1825–4 MARCH 1829

Louisa Adams made history – and controversy – by becoming the first foreign-born first lady, the only immigrant to bear the title of White House hostess until the 2016 presidential election of Donald Trump. Certainly, there have been comparisons between Melania and Louisa, but the former, unlike Trump, entered uncharted territory and faced unprecedented backlash over her identity.

Her story began in London, where she was born in 1775, just one year before the U.S. would claim its independence. Though her father was raised in the colonies, her mother was British-born, and Louisa's upbringing mirrored that of "young, pretty, wealthy English girls," writes Louisa Thomas in her biography of the first lady, *Louisa: The Extraordinary Life of Mrs. Adams*.[1]

Louisa remained in London, where she met John Quincy Adams while he was on a diplomatic mission on behalf of the U.S. government. Following their six-month courtship, the two were married there in 1797.[2]

In 1801, at the age of 26, Louisa arrived in the States, bringing with her the scandal of her European background. John Quincy's mother, former first lady Abigail Adams, known to be an outspoken and at times sharp-tongued woman, made her disapproval clear and labelled Louisa a "half-blood."[3]

Despite their strained relationship, like her mother-in-law, Louisa took an interest in politics during a time when women were expected to confine themselves to traditional roles and domestic activities. According to Thomas, Louisa would, at times, downplay her appetite for politics, writing "lengthy letters about political gossip" that moved "way beyond mainstream news of the day" before denying she had any interest in the subject at all.[4]

When President James Monroe appointed John Quincy Secretary of State in 1817, Louisa was brought further into political life, and both learned there were societal expectations that couldn't be ignored.

That started with making their first social calls to Congress members – a custom for newcomers. However, when the couple neglected their duty, feeling it was perhaps an unnecessary show of subordination, Louisa suffered social isolation, being cast out temporarily by the women of Washington. Realizing it had also impacted her husband's career, she wrote at the time that she "could have hardly imagined that a man's interests could be so dependent on his wife's manners."[5]

Having become aware that social gestures could wield great influence in Washington, Louisa began in 1819 what would become a tradition of hosting weekly tea parties, attracting visits from the very same women that once froze her out.[6] Her extroversion and charm became an advantage for her husband, and likely helped to offset his socially awkward nature during his campaign for the presidency.[7]

While she gained popularity, the controversy of Louisa's birthplace would never be laid to rest, and her parties served as ammunition for her critics,

12 FEBRUARY 1775 // Born in London to Joshua Johnson and an unknown mother

1797 // Meets John Quincy Adams on a diplomatic mission and marries him after a six-month courtship

1801 // Arrives in the U.S., aged 26

1817 // John Quincy appointed secretary of state

1819 // Louisa begins to host legendary tea parties in Washington

8 FEBRUARY 1825 // Hosts tea party that arguably secures Quincy's election

1827 // attacks on Louisa's European background worsen. An article about her biography appears in the *Philadelphia Evening Post*

1829 // John Quincy's presidency ends, they leave the White House

1831 // Quincy returns to the House of Representatives

1848 // Quincy dies of a heart attack

15 MAY 1852 // Louisa dies, also of a heart attack

who pointed to them as signs of her embrace of the old-world aristocracy and a desire for political clout.[8]

Her final and likely most important tea party was held on 8 February 1825. Andrew Jackson had just won not only the popular vote for the presidency but a plurality of electoral votes, leaving John Quincy in need of the majority of electoral votes to claim victory. It would all come down to the House of Representatives' decision the next day.

That night, according to John Quincy's diary, 67 representatives attended Louisa's soirée, in addition to "400 citizens and strangers."[9]

The following day, John Quincy was elected president. History gives much attention to Jackson's allegation of a "corrupt bargain" between House Speaker Henry Clay and John Quincy, but the power of Louisa's social influence, though it cannot be fully ascertained, certainly didn't hurt.[10]

In 1825, John Quincy was inaugurated, marking the start of Louisa's first ladyship. Again, her background was thrown into the spotlight. Historian L. H. Butterfield writes that the public began protesting not only her birthplace, but also the luxury in which she lived, accusing her of "aping royalty."[11]

The attacks worsened in 1827 when Jackson's supporters, seeking to advance his campaign for the next presidential election, insinuated that Louisa wasn't a real American.[12]

Taking matters into her own hands in a defensive show of guardianship over her image – and by extension, her husband's – Louisa wrote to her relatives, requesting evidence of her American lineage.[13] That year, the *Philadelphia Evening Post* printed an anonymously authored biography of Louisa in which the stated purpose was to prove her to be "the daughter of an American Republican Merchant."[14] Louisa's adversaries said there was no doubt it was her work.

To Louisa's detriment, the article backfired, having emphasized her time in Europe while highlighting her insecurities.[15] In retaliation, the *United States Telegraph*, a popular opposition

ABOVE: An engraving of John Quincy Adams seated in a library, 1826.

paper, launched a string of attacks against the first lady, mocking her for advertising her supposed "republican virtues and connections" and eventually claiming to hold the "truths" of her background.[16] The relentless vilification prompted Jackson to tell the publication's editor to leave Louisa alone, and so it began to back down.[17]

Though it was based in part on disparaging the first lady, Jackson's campaign for the presidency proved successful, and in 1829, John Quincy and Louisa exited the White House.

RACHEL DONELSON JACKSON

(1767–1828)

Rachel Jackson became the second first-lady-to-be to die before her husband took office, leaving Andrew Jackson a widower. While she would never take up a formal role of leadership within the White House, Rachel showed leadership within her personal life, making the daring decision to leave an abusive relationship when she met the president-to-be. The choice, though a necessary escape for Rachel, would follow her for the rest of her years, even colouring public perception of her husband's campaign.

Rachel was born in 1767, near modern-day Chatham, Virginia, and eventually moved with her family to Tennessee, marrying landowner Lewis Robards at age 18. Historian Harriet Chappell Owley describes Lewis as "a suspicious and jealous" man who "accused his wife of having affairs with the men boarders in his mother's home," despite "reports of wrongdoing on his part," including sleeping in the slave quarters with women, likely without their consent.[1]

In 1789, Rachel met Andrew Jackson, who was then a local lawyer, while on a trip to Natchez, a Spanish-controlled territory in West Florida. That year, Rachel left Lewis in a bold display of feminism that was, for its time, extraordinary, and married Andrew.

Ann Toplovich, executive director of the Tennessee Historical Society, writes in praise of Rachel, declaring her no victim but "a strong woman on the American frontier who at 21 years old decided to overthrow convention in order to leave her unhappy marriage and throw her lot in with the young, up and coming Andrew Jackson."[2]

To Rachel's surprise, perhaps, there was a wrinkle in the plan – Lewis had never finalized their divorce. In 1793, Lewis went after Rachel in court (despite the fact that he himself had already remarried) resulting in her conviction for adultery. For Rachel, the consequence would be a lifelong reputation stained by scandal. According to Emily Donelson, Andrew's niece, her uncle's marriage to Rachel was filled with love, and he found "his chief pleasure in her companionship, his greatest reward in her approval."[3] But the perceived shame of Rachel's past loomed over his presidential run in 1828, supplying his enemies with a stockpile of ammunition with which to smear his campaign.

"The effect on Rachel of being the object of insults and abuse was devastating," writes Owsley.[4] "The happy, fun-loving woman, saddened by the slanders withdrew from the unfriendly eyes of her persecutors."[5]

In awe of the uproar, William Berkeley Lewis, a friend of Andrew's, wrote in 1827 that the affair "had been represented to be a thousand times worse than it was."[6]

Buckling under the weight of the inevitable attacks, which ran rampant in the press, Rachel pleaded with Andrew to leave politics, intent on staying in Tennessee throughout her husband's term even after he was elected.[7] However, she eventually changed her mind, even buying a dress for the inauguration.[8]

In the wake of Andrew's election, the scars of Rachel's repeated denigration were evident in the

> "I saw myself, whom you have all guarded from outside criticism and surrounded with flattering delusions, as others see me, a poor old woman, suited for fashionable gaieties, a hindrance instead of helpmeet to the man I adore."

— RACHEL DONELSON JACKSON, 1828

words she reportedly told her niece upon hearing the gossip of other women: "Listening to them, it seemed as if a veil was lifted and I saw myself, whom you have all guarded from outside criticism and surrounded with flattering delusions, as others see me, a poor old woman, suited for fashionable gaieties, a hindrance instead of helpmeet to the man I adore."[9]

Months before Andrew's swearing-in, tragedy struck: Rachel died of a heart attack. Andrew insisted the cause was the toll of his opponents, but in truth Rachel had been experiencing heart trouble for three years.[10]

Emily, then 21 years old, was asked to take Rachel's place as the primary White House hostess, a role she filled until being dismissed during the Peggy Eaton affair, a scandal surrounding a cabinet member's wife whose private love life became public. The controversy caused much of Washington – including Emily – to spurn Peggy as a social outcast. Furious, and likely reminded of the tarnishing of his late wife's reputation, Andrew ousted Emily, and asked his adopted son's wife, Sarah Yorke Jackson, to step in.

Neither of Rachel's replacements would leave a lasting impact in their role as first lady.

ABOVE: The Hermitage, Andrew Jackson's plantation home, which was built on a more than 1,100-acre estate just outside of Nashville, Tennessee. Both the president and his wife, Rachel Jackson, are buried here.

OPPOSITE: Andrew Jackson gesturing at the Constitution.

HANNAH HOES VAN BUREN

(1783 – 1819)

Little is known about the life of Hannah Van Buren, which was cut short just 12 years after her marriage to Martin Van Buren, making him the third president to enter office as a widower.

Born in 1783 in Kinderhook, New York, her family didn't quite fit that of a woman who might have one day been a first lady: her father, Johannes Dircksen Goes, was a staunch Loyalist during the days of the Revolution, and one of the town's most fervent critics of independence.[1]

In 1807, just shy of her 24th birthday, Hannah married Martin, who was then a lawyer, in a clandestine ceremony held across the Hudson River in Catskill.[2] Notably, the two were first cousins, their union being the first and only to occur between a future president and his family member. Five years later, Martin was elected to the state senate and the couple moved to Albany.

Because he left Hannah out of his autobiography, details of their time together are practically non-existent. According to the White House Historical Association, "a gentleman of that day would not shame a lady by public references."[3]

Benjamin Butler, Van Buren's apprentice and New York's Democratic Party leader, wrote at the time that Hannah was "a woman of sweet nature but few intellectual gifts," who had "no ambitious desires."[4] Though Butler's description isn't all too flattering, those close to Hannah wrote glowingly of her warm demeanor. An account from her niece describes Hannah's "modest, even timid manner – her shrinking from observation, and her loving, gentle disposition."[5]

Church records indicate she considered religion an important matter. In *The Albany Argus*, a local semi-weekly newspaper, she was praised as "an ornament of the Christian faith."[6]

Hannah died in 1819, appearing to have contracted tuberculosis. Her obituary stated that her death was "severely felt by a numerous circle of relatives and friends."[7]

"In her last illness she was patient and resigned," it read.[8] "In the midst of life, with all that could make it worth possessing – esteemed and loved, happy in her family and friends – she was forced away."[9]

Martin never remarried, entering the White House in 1837 with his four bachelor sons. Abraham, the eldest, ended up marrying Angelica Singleton, an in-law of Dolley Madison who was still a prominent woman of Washington society.

During Martin's presidency, Angelica would serve as the White House hostess, taking Hannah's place and becoming part of a growing tradition of women who took up the torch for those who did not live to carry it.

ANNA TUTHILL SYMMES HARRISON

(1775–1864)

FIRST LADY: 4 MARCH 1841–4 APRIL 1841

Though, unlike several of her predecessors, Anna Harrison lived to take on the title of first lady, she never actually served in the role. William Henry Harrison's term was abruptly ended by his death one month after his inauguration, making her the first first lady to be widowed during her husband's administration.

Born in 1775 in Sussex County, New Jersey, Anna immediately distinguished her background from each of the first ladies before her by receiving a public education.[1] At age 19, she moved with her family to a settlement on the Ohio River, marrying William, then a military officer, in 1795.

Anna appears to have been fairly intellectual, having read political journals, though as Howard University history professor Edna Greene Medford notes, it isn't clear that she was a political person by nature.[2] In fact, Anna opposed her husband's campaign, stating after his 1840 election, "I wish that my husband's friends had left him where he is, happy and contented in retirement."[3]

As Medford describes her, "she was a reluctant first lady."[4]

In poor health and too ill to travel from their Ohio home to Washington for her husband's 1841 inauguration, Anna missed the event. Handing her duties off to daughter-in-law Jane Irvin Harrison, Anna planned to make the journey when road conditions improved.

Four weeks later, just as she was about to join William, she received notice that he had died of a cold that turned into pneumonia. Medford suspects his case was exacerbated by exhaustion coupled with advancing age, as he was already 68.[5]

Until now, a president's death while in office had been unprecedented. Under Anna's new status as a widow, Congress awarded her $25,000 and the franking privilege, which allowed her to send mail for free.

Though historians can only speculate about how she would have fulfilled her role as first lady, Anna *did* use her clout after William's death to persuade his vice president and successor, John Tyler, to appoint her family members to political posts, thereby demonstrating a small measure of influence.

> "I wish that my husband's friends had left him where he is, happy and contented in retirement."
>
> – ANNA TUTHILL SYMMES HARRISON, 1840

LETITIA CHRISTIAN TYLER

(1790–1842)

FIRST LADY: 4 APRIL 1841–10 SEPTEMBER 1842

By the time her husband, John Tyler, became president in 1841 following William Henry Harrison's sudden death, Letitia Tyler had already been partially paralyzed for two years by a stroke. Given that her health left her confined to a chair, she was, like other first ladies, forced to hand over her role of White House hostess to a substitute – in this case, daughter-in-law Priscilla Cooper Tyler.

Born in 1790, Letitia hailed from New Kent County, Virginia, the birthplace of Martha Washington and a state that a total of five first ladies called home. In 1813, she married John, an attorney and member of the Virginia House of Delegates.

Letitia did not wholeheartedly support John's entry into national politics, feeling that it too often pulled him away from home and family.[1] In 1818, she urged him to exit Congress and instead focus on practicing law and spending more time with his children, but for John, politics held greater appeal.[2]

During his vice presidency, the couple lived in Williamsburg, as this role was not as well developed and involved as it is today. Though Letitia was in poor health when she learned of her husband's rise to the presidency, she decided to move into the White House for care, though she could not engage in the social duties traditionally undertaken by first ladies.

Still, according to historian Edith Mayo, a curator emerita for political history in the National Museum of American History, Letitia delivered directions from the second floor of the White House, where she spent nearly all of her time, with the exception of her attendance at the wedding of one of her seven children.[3] As Priscilla describes her, Letitia was "the most entirely unselfish person you can imagine" who "attends to and regulates all the household affairs and all so quietly that you can't tell when she does it."[4]

In contemporary journalist Laura Holloway's *Ladies of the White House*, a series of biographical sketches published in 1870, she writes that though Letitia didn't venture outside, she was able "to converse with visitors on current topics intelligently," and spend her time sewing, knitting, reading or with family.[5]

In Holloway's words, though Letitia appeared to be the sort of woman who "could easily have impressed her power upon what is termed society had she so desired," she had no inclination to do so, and instead "modestly shrank from all notoriety and evaded the public eye as much as possible."[6]

Taylor Stoermer, a public history lecturer at Johns Hopkins University's Museum Studies program, notes that Letitia's limitations due to her health raise questions over the definition of a first lady – could the title only signify one's marriage to the president, or must it always entail a list of responsibilities?[7] Without a formal definition, it remains a matter of debate.

Regardless of Letitia's condition, Stoermer also suspects that because of her withdrawn nature, she would have taken a less-involved approach to the role even if she hadn't had the stroke.

Halfway through John's term, Letitia died in 1842, having spent less than two years in her role. At age 51, she became the first and youngest first lady to die in the White House.

JULIA GARDINER TYLER

(1820–89)

Though she served as first lady for less than a year as John Tyler's presidency came to a close, Julia Tyler was perhaps the first woman to obtain celebrity status in the role, harnessing the power of the press and taking ownership of her public image.

The so-called "Rose of Long Island" was born in New York City in 1820, making her first foray into the spotlight at age 19 when she appeared in an ad for a local department store. Though her name wasn't used, her nickname was printed, featuring an image of a rose, a clear nod to the young socialite.[1] At the time, public exposure for an unmarried woman of Julia's age was considered a scandal, leading her family to temporarily whisk her away to Europe while the controversy died down.[2]

By 1841, she returned to the United States, and was courted by John a year later, merely months after the death of his wife. The president, 30 years her senior, was relentless in his marriage proposals to Julia despite her initial rejection of his offer. In 1844, they were married.

For Julia, appearance was of crucial importance, and her image in the White House was marked by extravagance. As writer at the time Jessie Frémont observed, Julia was the subject of a measure of derision for using "finer horses than those of the Russian minister," and for receiving guests while seated in a large armchair, dressed in a long, velvet purple gown with "three feathers in her hair."[3]

The feathers – echoing the insignia of the Prince of Wales – may have been a sign of European influence, in addition to Julia's formation of her own "court" of sorts: a flock of ladies-in-waiting who followed her everywhere, dressed in white and dubbed her "vestal virgins."[4] According to Frémont, Julia's style was "much commented on by the elders who had seen other Presidents' wives take their state more easily."[5]

The first lady ensured that the president also received red-carpet treatment, requesting that "Hail to the Chief" be played on official occasions to announce his arrival.[6] She, too, had her own music, "The Julia Waltzes," which were named in her honour, a badge of recognition she sought to publicize.[7]

Though historical accounts of Julia's time in the White House focus primarily on her social status and style, she did, in fact, wield a limited degree of political influence, as evidenced by her effort to lobby for the 1845 annexation of Texas.

Her efforts included appearing at the Capitol to hear debates on the matter and disseminating copies of her husband's proposal to approve the annexation via a joint resolution requiring a majority of both houses.[8] Julia used her charm to rally the necessary support among lawmakers, even managing to win the endorsement of Supreme Court Justice John McLean – one of her former admirers – who made a toast to "Texas and Tyler" at a dinner in Washington one night.[9]

Again, the press noticed Julia, crediting her campaign in a political cartoon depicting the

> ## "I intend to do something in the way of entertaining that shall be the admiration and talk of all the Washington world."

– JULIA GARDINER TYLER, 1844

president at a fork in the road, one direction labelled "Texas" and the other the "White House."[10] Julia is shown several steps away on the path to Texas, appearing to encourage her husband to follow her lead.[11]

In the weeks before John's term ended, Julia held a "Grand Finale Ball" attended by 3,000 guests who consumed nearly 100 bottles of champagne[12] as she danced with foreign ambassadors and government officials.[13]

The lavish and lively soirée was a testament both to Julia's hostess abilities and the popularity she attained during her relatively brief time in the White House. She left behind a legacy primarily as a skilled entertainer who commanded public recognition.[14]

OPPOSITE: A photograph believed to be of Julia Tyler, which would have made her the first first lady to be photographed.

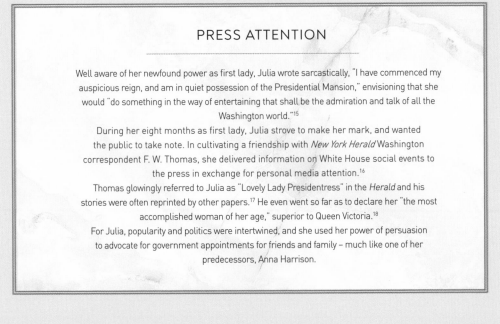

PRESS ATTENTION

Well aware of her newfound power as first lady, Julia wrote sarcastically, "I have commenced my auspicious reign, and am in quiet possession of the Presidential Mansion," envisioning that she would "do something in the way of entertaining that shall be the admiration and talk of all the Washington world."[15]

During her eight months as first lady, Julia strove to make her mark, and wanted the public to take note. In cultivating a friendship with *New York Herald* Washington correspondent F. W. Thomas, she delivered information on White House social events to the press in exchange for personal media attention.[16]

Thomas glowingly referred to Julia as "Lovely Lady Presidentress" in the *Herald* and his stories were often reprinted by other papers.[17] He even went so far as to declare her "the most accomplished woman of her age," superior to Queen Victoria.[18]

For Julia, popularity and politics were intertwined, and she used her power of persuasion to advocate for government appointments for friends and family – much like one of her predecessors, Anna Harrison.

SARAH CHILDRESS POLK

(1803–91)

FIRST LADY 4 MARCH 1845–4 MARCH 1849

Upon her husband's election, Sarah Polk emerged as one of the most powerful women of her time, cleverly wielding influence within the confines of a patriarchal society through her strategic political partnership with the president.

Sarah was born in 1803 in Murfreesboro, Tennessee, and met James Polk during his time as the clerk of the state Senate. The two married in 1824 after he was elected to the state legislature. They never had any children, which set them apart from the norms of the day. Amy Greenberg, a professor of history and women's studies at Pennsylvania State University and the author of *Lady First: The World of First Lady Sarah Polk*, speculates that this was an intentional decision as John was deeply involved in politics and Sarah had no interest in playing housewife.[1]

After their wedding, James remarked that she impressed his relatives by "display[ing] a great deal of spice and more independence of judgement than was fitting in one woman," standing shoulder-to-shoulder with a college-educated husband eight years her senior.[2]

It appears James even helped to encourage Sarah's rejection of household duties. When she suggested during his time in Congress that she remain at their home in Tennessee, he reportedly responded, "Why? If it burns down, we can live without it."[3]

Further breaking from tradition, just before James was elected president in 1844, she declared, "If I get to the White House ... I will neither keep house nor make butter," in response to a remark that challenger Henry Clay's wife was a skilled homemaker.[4]

As first lady, Sarah won the public's respect through her image as a devout Presbyterian who practiced a strict adherence to the Sabbath, embraced modesty, and avoided drinking and dancing – in stark contrast to the flamboyance of her predecessor, Julia Tyler.

Recognizing Sarah's religiosity, the *Nashville Union*, a contemporary newspaper, praised her "salutary influence," calling it a rebuke of "the conduct of those ladies who professing godliness, nevertheless dishonor its profession by their eager participation in the follies and amusements of the world."[5]

In the White House, Sarah wore various hats, acting as the president's assistant and communications director, reviewing news coverage, saving articles of interest, and editing certain of his speeches.[6,7] Greenberg notes that it is evident in letters sent to the president that others understood the extent of her involvement in his administration, addressing their messages to both James and Sarah.[8]

Later in life, James attested to the closeness of their alliance, stating, "None but Sarah knew so intimately my private affairs."[9]

Sarah was especially vocal in her support of the Mexican-American War and championed the "Manifest Destiny" concept on which it was predicated, proclaiming that God willed the U.S. to expand its borders. While some within the Whig Party viewed the invasion of Mexico as an unethical land-grab, Sarah lobbied Congress members to

4 SEPTEMBER 1803 // Born to Joel Childress and Elizabeth Whitsett in Murfreesboro, Tennessee

1824 // Married James Knox Polk, a Tennessee clerk

1825 // Elected to the United States Congress, Polk moves to Washington, leaving Sarah in Tennessee

1826 // Sarah moves to Washington to aid her husband's political career

1844 // James Polk elected president

1848 // Polk's presidency ends. He dies four months later from cholera at 45 years old

1850 // Sarah Polk returns to her cotton plantation

1860 // On the outbreak of the Civil War, Sarah declares herself neutral and welcomes both Union and Confederate military leaders to her home. She later admits she sympathized with the South

14 AUGUST 1891 // Dies in Nashville, Tennessee

"If I get to the White House... I will neither keep house nor make butter."

– SARAH CHILDRESS POLK, 1844

continue backing the war after it began in 1846, holding White House receptions to which veterans were invited.[10]

While she was a feminist in her own right, Sarah was also well aware that in Washington she operated in a male-dominated arena, and she often avoided challenging the authority of those within it by masking her own views as those of the president, prefacing her opinions with "Mr. Polk believes..." rather than taking ownership of her positions.[11]

As Greenberg writes, "she set a model of conservative female power that grew and flourished in the century after her death, and which actively shapes our current political moment."[12] Women who would later rise to power, including hardline conservative activist Phyllis Schlafly and first ladies Nancy Reagan and Ivanka Trump, are all "political heirs" of Sarah's, Greenberg states.[13]

However, Sarah opposed suffrage and did not attend the 1848 Seneca Falls Convention, believing that voting rights were unnecessary for women. In this sense, her motivation to influence politics was self-serving – she already had the power she desired as first lady, and wasn't interested in helping others climb the ladder. She also stood firmly against the abolition of slavery, arguing the South would crumble without it.

Though Sarah only spent one term as first lady, she forged a new path for Washington women seeking to shape politics while appearing to maintain the status quo, quietly exerting influence and amassing power within a male-centric government that still sought to deny them equality.

OPPOSITE: Sarah Polk seated next to her unofficially adopted daughter and longtime friend, Sallie Jetton.

MARGARET MACKALL SMITH TAYLOR

(1790–1842)

FIRST LADY: 4 MARCH 1849–9 JULY 1850

On the heels of the first ladyships of Julia Tyler and Sarah Polk, there could not have been a starker contrast than Margaret Taylor, a woman who swore off politics, shied away from media attention, and preferred that her husband not be elected at all.

Born in Calvert County, Maryland, in 1788, Margaret met Zachary Taylor in 1809 and married him the following year. Zachary was then a young army lieutenant pursuing what would become a 40-year military career that earned him his trademark nickname "Old Rough and Ready." Margaret followed where his career led, moving from post to post and embracing frontier life – a change of pace from the life offered by the couple's aristocratic backgrounds.

As historian Elizabeth Lorelei Thacker-Estrada writes in her essay on antebellum-era presidential wives, "True Women," Margaret had earned the reputation of a "tough, careworn pioneer woman and peripatetic military wife transplanted from her cultured eastern roots."[1]

Her reluctance to serve as first lady echoed that of Martha Washington, as both had eagerly looked forward to retirement on their plantations, and felt a tinge of resentment upon realizing they would instead be thrust into the spotlight and burdened by public duties.

Opposing Zachary's candidacy, Margaret griped to her relatives that it "was a plot to deprive her of his society, and shorten his life by unnecessary care and responsibility."[2] However, when it came time to serve after her husband's inauguration in 1849, Margaret arrived at the White House within days.[3]

Still unwilling to fulfill her new role in its totality, Margaret passed it off to her 23-year-old daughter, Betty, who joined a tradition of surrogate first ladies, presiding over social functions as hostess-in-chief. Meanwhile, Margaret spent much of her time in an upper room of the White House, where she received visitors, claiming to have been handicapped by her "delicate health," though her explanations were vague.[4]

Decades later, writers joked that the first lady must have stowed herself away in the room with a pipe, but close friends and family noted that she abhorred the smell of tobacco, suggesting the rumours were more likely a jab at her wilful solitude.[5]

According to Thacker-Estrada, like most antebellum first ladies, Margaret was "seldom mentioned in official or public records and rarely discussed in newspapers," which left historians lacking the depth of information left by certain of her predecessors.[6] Of course, her avoidance of her role from the outset would not have helped to place her in a position of high visibility.

Margaret also avoided sitting for portraits or photographs, even maintaining a closely guarded image at her husband's deathbed, where she covered her face with an oversized handkerchief, leaving an engraver who had wanted to sell images of the scene baffled as to what she looked like.[7]

Albeit the first lady had, at times, eschewed her

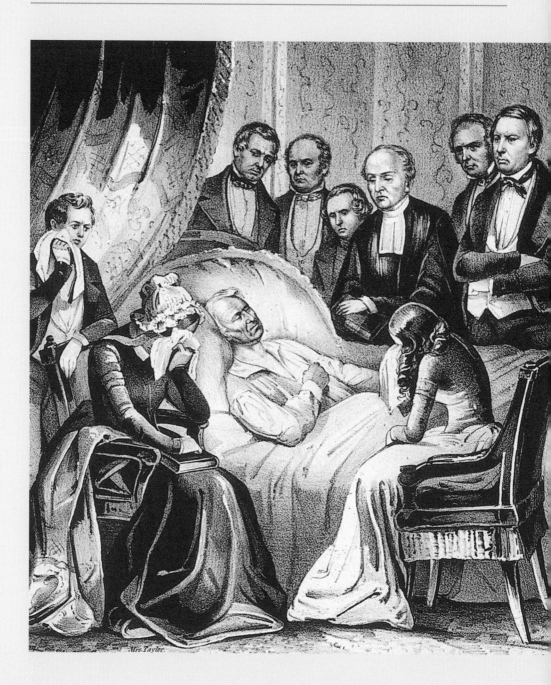

Mrs. Tayler.

role, she earned the respect of the president, who once told Democratic Senator Jefferson Davis, a Mexican war hero, "You know my wife was as much of a soldier as I was."[8]

In 1850, Margaret's ominous prediction that her husband's life would be cut short proved true. Less than two years into his term, Zachary fell ill and died of cholera, shortly after the couple marked their 40th anniversary.[9] The tragedy made Margaret the first first lady to serve during the death of a president, as Anna Harrison had not yet arrived in Washington when William Henry Harrison died in 1841.

Margaret died just two years later, reportedly without ever having mentioned the White House again.[10] In one final sign of her privacy in the media even in death, a *New York Times* obituary referred to her as "Mrs. General Taylor," opting to leave out her full name.[11]

A RARE POLITICAL INTERVENTION

When it came to political influence, there is little evidence Margaret wielded much power – certainly not to the extent of Sarah Polk. To her credit, however, she appears to have persuaded the president to appoint to the post of attorney general Reverdy Johnson, a Whig Party senator from her home state, whose wife was coincidentally her cousin.[12]

Margaret additionally took part in an administrative effort to entertain Whig leaders who felt unappreciated after backing her husband's candidacy. In rare moments, it seemed, she could wade into political matters.[13]

ABIGAIL POWERS FILLMORE

(1798–1853)

FIRST LADY: 9 JULY 1850–4 MARCH 1853

Abigail Powers Fillmore had not expected to become first lady, but following President Zachary Taylor's death in 1850, as the wife of Vice President Millard Fillmore, she stepped up.

Though hesitant to embrace her new position, routinely avoiding social functions, which her daughter would attend in her place, Abigail brought an insatiable intellect to the White House, and is credited with the creation of its library.

Born in 1798 in upstate New York, Abigail's curiosity was instilled in her from a young age. At 16, she became a schoolteacher, the most popular occupation for first ladies-to-be and one of the only paid professions that employed women at the time.[1] In 1819, she met Millard while an instructor at the private New Hope Academy where he had enrolled. Having grown up impoverished with, as he recalled, "no access to books" aside from his school materials and his father's library, which "consisted only of a Bible, hymn book, and almanac," Millard took charge of his own learning.[2]

While his teacher, Abigail inspired him to continue in his studies, playing a key role in preparing him for an accomplished political life by fostering his education. As historian Robert Rayback writes in his biography of the president-to-be, the year they met, "Abigail's love had spurred him on to higher ambitions, so now her faith and his responsibility stirred him to greater activity."[3]

They married seven years later, in 1826.

Millard's political career took flight, climbing the ranks from New York State assemblyman to congressman to comptroller of New York before becoming vice president, having also become a successful lawyer. Rising from humble beginnings, his triumphs are a testament not only to Millard's character, but to his wife, who championed his education.

While living in Buffalo, the couple cultivated an expansive home library, described by one of the city's newspapers as "a local attraction."[4] Historian Betty Boyd Caroli, the first to write an extensive biography of the women *First Ladies*, in 1987, dubbed the Fillmore house "a gathering place for Buffalo's literati."[5]

Aside from Abigail's part in building the White House's library, as Caroli writes, upon Millard's rise to power, "she was left to look after seating arrangements at dinner parties," indicating she did not wield political influence.[6] Nevertheless, according to one Washington journalist, she was "remarkably well informed," following political developments and acting as the president's sounding board.[7] As Harriet Scott, the wife of then-Congressman Solomon Haven, wrote, Millard treated Abigail with the courtesy, "like that which a man usually bestows upon a guest," never taking "any important step without her counsel and advice."[8]

Less than one month after the end of her husband's presidential term, Abigail died of what was likely pneumonia.[9] Though she was not politically influential, Abigail's contribution to her husband's education laid the groundwork for his eventual rise to the presidency.

JANE MEANS APPLETON PIERCE

(1806-63)

FIRST LADY: 4 MARCH 1853–4 MARCH 1857

Bearing the everlasting anguish of the loss of her three children, a lifelong hatred for politics, and a growing resentment toward her husband for having staked his career in a field he once vowed to abandon, Jane Pierce's first ladyship would be practically non-existent as she withdrew into an understandably depressive state.

Born in Hampton, New Hampshire, in 1806, Jane was well acquainted with sorrow from a young age, her brother John and father Jesse, a Congregationalist pastor, having died while she was just a teenager. At age 28, she married Franklin Pierce, who was then an attorney and congressman. From the start, the couple were a painfully evident mismatch, Jane's sombre demeanour and intense introversion clashing with Franklin's youthful exuberance.[1] As historian Roy Nichols writes in his biography, *Franklin Pierce: Young Hickory of the Granite Hills*, Jane "was shy, retiring, frail and tubercular, well-bred in the straightest sect of New England theocracy with a host of substantial and aristocratic connections."[2] Meanwhile, her husband was "buoyant, vain, social, at home in political caucus and tavern, a son of the frontier."[3]

"They were ill-mated," Nichols adds, "but for thirty years they lived together, he dividing himself between politics and law, giving her a very real affection and love which made her the center of his thoughtful attention."[4] Though they held fast to their commitment to each other, diverging personas and differing values would inevitably prove a lasting strain on their union.

After their marriage ceremony, Jane joined Franklin in Washington, where she found the lifestyle insufferable; she recoiled at its society in which there "was nothing to do but talk, think and act politics."[5] Meanwhile, she remained concerned by the culture of heavy drinking among politicians,[6] which would certainly have been of no benefit to her husband, who drank to excess. Throughout her adult life, Jane made a habit of excusing herself from social engagements involving her husband by citing personal illnesses, potentially seeking to distance herself from the life he had chosen.[7] Pregnant with her first child, Jane retreated to Massachusetts to stay with her relatives, allowing her a temporary break from the city.[8]

Her son died three days after he was born in 1836, marking the first of several tragedies that would befall the Pierces. The following year, as Franklin's reputation grew, he dived further into political affairs and was elected to the Senate, prompting Jane to return to Washington once more. She hated it. "Oh, how I wish he was out of political life," she wrote in 1837 to her aunt-in-law, Abigail Kent Means. "How much better it would be for him on every account!"[9]

Aware of Jane's disdain for his career, Franklin decided to step down from his seat in 1842, albeit he had made himself an up-and-comer in Congress.[10] The year after, the Pierces' second son died of typhus at age four.[11]

In 1846, President James Polk offered Franklin the position of attorney general, but he declined,

fretting it might be more than his increasingly sickly wife could bear. "Besides, you know that Mrs. Pierce's health while at Washington was very delicate," he stated.[12] He also refused to run for governor of New Hampshire.[13]

For the moment, Franklin had drifted from politics, and it seemed Jane's wishes might have finally been granted. Franklin even promised her that he would not seek the presidency in 1852 and assured her he would instead remove his name from the shortlist of candidates.[14] But that year, he became the Democratic Party nominee. Shocked, Jane fainted when she learned the news.[15]

Jane took no part in her husband's campaign, fervently praying it would fail. The couple's remaining son, Benny, then 11 years old, shared in his mother's displeasure, writing to her, "I hope he won't be elected for I shall not like to be at Washington and I know you would not either."[16]

Upon learning of his overwhelming electoral victory, Franklin savoured the win despite the misgivings of the new first lady, who would be pulled back again into public life.[17] However, the celebration was short-lived. In 1853, two months before Inauguration Day, the Pierces were involved in a train accident in which their car lurched off the tracks. Though the couple survived, Benny, just shy of his 12th birthday, was struck on the head with a scrap of metal that killed him instantly in a gruesome scene that played out before his parents' eyes.[18]

A witness, identified by New Hampshire's *Manchester Mirror* as the Reverend Mr. Fuller, recalled that Jane's "agony [passed] beyond any description."[19]

"She could shed no tears, but, overcome with grief, uttered such affecting words as I can never forget," he said.[20] "It was Mrs. Pierce, the lady of the President-elect; and near her in the ruin of shivered wood and iron, lay a more terrible ruin – her only son, one minute before so beautiful, so full of life and hope."[21]

Neither Jane nor Franklin would recover from the loss.

Jane, who had been raised a strict Calvinist, believed God had willed her son's death so that the newly elected president could devote his attention to his career.[22] Grief-stricken and spiralling into depression, she was absent from his inauguration, and while in the White House, stowed herself away in upstairs rooms, earning the nickname, "the shadow in the White House."[23] Jane undertook virtually no public role.

Much of her time in mourning was spent penning letters to Benny, one of which was written less than three weeks after his death:

> When I have told you dear boy ["]how much you depended on me, and felt that you could not do without me" – I did not say too, how much I depended on you.
> … Now I am at home again dear boy – oh what anguish was mine on returning without you, and feeling that it must still be so, while I live – to see your little bed that you loved so much –
> and which I look at many times in the day, and at night feel as if I must see it out again and the clothes turned down for you –
> and unconsciously look in the morning for it and you – and listen for your bright cheerful voice."[24]

For two years, the first lady neither appeared at public functions nor received guests, and arranged for each of the White House's state rooms to be outfitted with permanent mourning bunting.[25] Entrenched in her sorrow, she partook in séances in a desperate attempt to reach her son, and sought solace in her faith.[26]

Many of her duties were passed on to her aunt-in-law and to Secretary of War Jefferson Davis's wife, Varina Howell Davis.[27]

Jane's first ladyship, remarkable only in its misfortunes, would leave her successors no meaningful legacy.

OPPOSITE: Sisters Margaretta, Kate, and Leah Fox, pictured from left to right. Margaretta and Kate in particular are credited with the birth of Spiritualism. Jane Pierce sought their help in communicating with her deceased son, Benny.

SPIRITUALISM IN THE WHITE HOUSE

While it still has followers today, Spiritualism was at its peak in the Victorian age. With its beginning in 1840s New York State, the movement's followers believe that spirits of the dead speak through mediums, often during a séance. The spirits communicate through raps and thumps, responding to questions and statements from the medium. The movement has been controversial, as those who wish to consult mediums are often vulnerable and grief-stricken, seeking any kind of comfort for their loss.[28]

The idea that Benny's spirit could be contacted led Jane to consult a pair of famous Spiritualists, Kate and Margaret Fox.[29] The Fox sisters were a sensation – their public séances attracted celebrity fans and they travelled the world. After consulting the Fox sisters, Jane's grief reportedly lifted to a degree, as she was visited in her dreams by her son's spirit. In 1888, the Fox sisters confessed to fraud and then quickly recanted the confession – but it was too late for their reputation, and they never regained the trust of the public.[30]

HARRIET REBECCA LANE JOHNSTON

(1830–1903)

FIRST LADY: 4 MARCH 1857–4 MARCH 1861

For a White House that had been visited by more than its fair share of sorrow and draped in permanent mourning bunting under the Pierce administration, Harriet Lane was a breath of fresh air, fostering a thriving social environment under President James Buchanan's politically unpopular leadership.

As his niece, Harriet was chosen to fill the position of first lady since he was a bachelor throughout his tenure, remaining the only commander-in-chief to serve while single.

As a young man, Buchanan had been engaged to Anne Coleman, a woman with whom he had fallen in love while working as a lawyer in Lancaster, Pennsylvania. Before the wedding, for reasons that remain unclear, Anne broke off the engagement. Shortly after, she died, possibly by suicide. Devastated, James resigned himself to lifelong bachelorhood.[1]

Harriet was herself no stranger to tragedy, being orphaned by the death of her mother at age nine and the loss of father two years later. Because she shared a close relationship with her uncle, whom she called "Nunc," James took Harriet under his wing and become a father figure during her formative years.[2]

Their closeness continued into Harriet's adulthood, when James invited her on a trip to London in 1854 during his time as secretary of state. According to writer and historian Mary Simmerson Cunningham Logan, Harriet's "surpassing brightness and loveliness seemed to make a deep impression" on Queen Victoria, who honored her with an official title typically given only to the wife of an ambassador.[3] As Logan stated, in that moment, "the youthful American girl became one of the leading ladies of the Diplomatic Corps of Saint James."[4]

Just 27 at the time of James's inauguration in 1857, Harriet assumed her role with an energy and enthusiasm that had been missing from her recent predecessors. At times, this approach would clash with the orthodoxy of her uncle, who embraced a more buttoned-down approach to life in the White House.

Among historians, Harriet's popularity, which soared to a celebrity status, has been likened to that of Dolley Madison, one of Washington's all-star hostesses who remained a matriarch long after exiting the White House. Harriet's image was further bolstered by a burgeoning press that finally began covering first ladies, fawning over her as the administration's "Democratic Queen."[5]

As first lady, Harriet filled the White House with the fanfare of parties and elegant dinners, managing, as the wife of a contemporary Alabama senator wrote, "to keep the surface of society in Washington serene and smiling, though the fires of a volcano raged in the under-political world."[6]

That volcano was the Civil War, the beginnings of which were brewing during James's tenure, as tensions between the North and the South reached a fever pitch.

Sara Pryor, a Confederate loyalist and friend of Harriet, also took note of her seemingly partisan

included Native Americans, some of whom thanked her by naming their daughters "Harriet."[9]

Recognition of the first lady was illustrated also by the naming of a ship in her honour by the now-disbanded U.S. Revenue Cutter Service. The vessel would eventually join Union naval forces in the Civil War before being captured by Confederates. Throughout history, only two other first ladies have enjoyed the prestige of having naval equipment bear their name.[10]

Aside from her advocacy for the arts, for which she was celebrated, perhaps the most significant accomplishment of Harriet's first ladyship came when she presided over the Prince of Wales' visit to Washington in 1860. By doing so he become the first heir of the British throne to enter the U.S., let alone stay in the White House. According to former Pennsylvania Historical Association President Homer Rosenberger, it signalled "a new day" in English-American relations.[11]

The following year, both Harriet and James would leave the White House mere months before the U.S. spiralled into the Civil War, a conflict for which certain critics would blame the departing president. Despite the political turmoil that plagued her years as first lady, Harriet made her mark by currying public favour in the face of the immense national strife that was about to erupt.

attitude in public, attributing it to the first lady's ability to befriend all with whom she crossed paths. "Always courteous, always in place, silent whenever it was possible to be silent, watchful, and careful, she made no enemies, was betrayed in no entangling alliances and was involved in no contretemps of any kind," she wrote.[7]

Though a skilled hostess, it is evident that Harriet attempted to exercise a measure of political influence as well, acting on appeals for assistance from members of the public who felt underrepresented by their government.[8] That

ABOVE LEFT: An engraving of James Buchanan c. 1860.

OPPOSITE: James Buchanan's niece, Harriet Lane, who took on the duties of the first lady since the president never married.

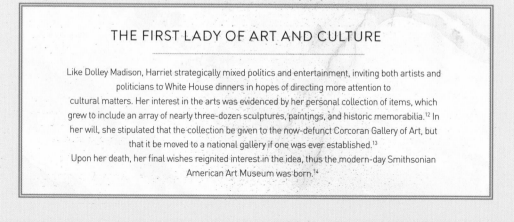

THE FIRST LADY OF ART AND CULTURE

Like Dolley Madison, Harriet strategically mixed politics and entertainment, inviting both artists and politicians to White House dinners in hopes of directing more attention to cultural matters. Her interest in the arts was evidenced by her personal collection of items, which grew to include an array of nearly three-dozen sculptures, paintings, and historic memorabilia.[12] In her will, she stipulated that the collection be given to the now-defunct Corcoran Gallery of Art, but that it be moved to a national gallery if one was ever established.[13]

Upon her death, her final wishes reignited interest in the idea, thus the modern-day Smithsonian American Art Museum was born.[14]

MARY TODD LINCOLN

(1818 – 82)

FIRST LADY: 4 MARCH 1861–15 APRIL 1865

Mary Lincoln, one of history's most infamous first ladies, seemed to achieve her tragic status largely through circumstances outside of her control. The deaths of three of her children coupled with the assassination of her husband before her very eyes sent Mary spiralling from an already fragile emotional state into paralyzing grief from which she made no recovery. As a result, her legacy is defined far more by her erratic behaviour than her contribution to the development of Abraham Lincoln's political career.

Born in Lexington, Kentucky, in 1818, Mary developed a reputation at a young age for her temperament, which shifted without warning. As her longtime friend Margaret Stuart once observed, Mary was "much like an April day, sunning all over with laughter one moment, the next crying as though her heart would break."[1]

Despite her turbulent disposition, which may have been the product of bipolar disorder, Mary was a talented student as well as a skilled seamstress and horsewoman.[2] Combined with her natural beauty and quick wit, she had no trouble attracting eligible men in her youth, including politicians.[3]

In 1842, she married Abraham, an attorney who had previously broken off the engagement, perhaps indicating their relationship was strained. Shortly after they tied the knot, he described the wedding to a friend as "a profound wonder."[4]

For all of history's attention to Mary's demeanour, she did, in fact, help to drive her husband's 1860 presidential run. Like Mary, Abe, too, fell into melancholic bouts, but she lifted him up, according to his law partner, John Stuart[5] "Lincoln is a gloomy man – a sad man," Stuart noted.[6] "His wife made him President. She had the fire – will and ambition – Lincoln's talent and his wife's ambition did the deed."[7]

As Abe campaigned, Mary proved herself to be one of his primary advocates, making herself available for interviews with the press, arranging tours of their Illinois home, and advising Abe on his competitors, some of which were her former suitors.[8]

As historian Jean Baker writes in her 1989 biography of the first lady-to-be, the day after Abe's nomination was confirmed, Mary began "using up all the ink she had purchased" to write letters to potential supporters in an effort to clarify her husband's positions.[9] Upon receiving news of his election, Abe suggested he perceived the victory as a joint accomplishment, declaring to his wife, "Mary, Mary, we are elected!"[10]

At first, Mary's first ladyship, from her prowess as a hostess to her redecoration of the mansion, was met with praise as she lived up to each of the role's traditional expectations. In the early months of Abe's presidency, she enjoyed favourable media coverage from *Leslie's* magazine, which applauded her "exquisite taste" and referred to her as "our fair 'Republican Queen.'"[11] However, Mary's image changed as her mental state gradually began to decline, and the start of the Civil War in 1861 served only to intensify her distress.

13 DECEMBER 1818 // Born in Lexington, Kentucky, fourth child of Robert and Eliza Parker Todd

5 JULY 1825 // Her mother dies following childbirth

1 NOVEMBER 1826 // Her father remarries to Elizabeth Humphreys. They go on to have nine children

4 NOVEMBER 1842 // Marries Abraham Lincoln. They go on to have four children

1 FEBRUARY 1850 // Her son Edward dies aged 3 years and 11 months

6 NOVEMBER 1860 // Abraham Lincoln is elected 16th president of the United States

4 MARCH 1861 // Attends her husband's first inauguration and inaugural ball in Washington

20 FEBRUARY 1862 // Her son William dies in the White House

4 MARCH 1865 // Attends her husband's second inauguration

14 APRIL 1865 // Witnesses the assassination of her husband

22 MAY 1865 // Leaves Washington to live in Chicago, Illinois

15 JULY 1871 // Her son Tad dies aged 18

20 MAY 1875 // Mary is committed to an asylum in Batavia, Illinois, by her only surviving child, Robert

16 JULY 1882 // Dies aged 63 at her sister's home in Springfield

ABOVE: A portrait of Mary Lincoln dressed in mourning attire.

Aware that certain of Mary's relatives enlisted as "rebels," her detractors spread rumours that she secretly harboured Confederate sympathies, even though she had publicly allied herself with the Union cause. Though it had no credibility, the hearsay wasn't always easy to dismiss. At one point, Republican politician Thurlow Weed, one of Abe's prominent supporters, reportedly claimed – falsely, of course – that Mary had been outcast from Washington as a "traitor."[12]

In 1862, Mary was faced with tragedy over the death of her 11-year-old son Will, marking her second loss of a child. Her other son, Edward died in 1850, just shy of his fourth birthday. Jason Emerson, historian and author of *The Madness of Mary Lincoln,* believes it to have been a catalyst in her mental deterioration, describing her pain as "incapacitating" and noting she sequestered herself in her room for weeks.[13]

However, certain of her actions while grieving only worsened her image: she spent excessively on mourning attire and special jewelry, prompting questions over the true depth of her sorrow. Shopping sprees would become a compulsive habit of Mary's, leaving her at one

> ## "I would rather marry a good man, a man of mind, with a hope and bright prospects ahead for position, fame and power than to marry all the houses, gold and bones in the world."
>
> – MARY TODD LINCOLN, 1842

point in a $27,000 hole of debt – more than her husband's annual salary.[14]

Stories of Mary's erratic behaviour began to circulate as close friends alleged that she was prone to erupting into tantrums to get her way. According to Julia Taft, whose brothers were tutored at the White House alongside Mary's children, the first lady's wrath did not subside until her wishes were granted.[15] "Mrs. Lincoln wanted what she wanted when she wanted it and no substitute! And as far as we know she always had it, including a President of the United States."[16]

While in the White House, Abe confided in Orville Browning, who served for a short time as a senator from Illinois, about his concerns over Mary's behaviour. According to Browning, Abe "was constantly under great apprehension lest his wife should do something which would bring him into disgrace."[17]

In 1865, tragedy struck Mary once again six months after Abe's re-election when he was assassinated before her very eyes by Confederate sympathizer John Wilkes Booth while attending a play at Ford's Theatre in Washington. Tasked with finding a new home for herself at the age of 47, Mary left the White House just five weeks later.[18]

Having become fixated on money, she felt the roughly $35,000 estate left to her and her two remaining sons was inadequate, arguing that Congress owed her more given the circumstances.[19] Eventually, she was granted a $3,000 pension, which was later increased to $5,000.[20] Among lawmakers, the controversy outlived Mary, fueled in part by unprecedented questions over the treatment of a president's widow in the aftermath of his murder.[21]

In 1871, Mary's mental state appeared to take its defeating blow upon the death of her 18-year-old son Tad, with whom she shared a close bond. By 1875, her remaining son, Robert, had her temporarily committed to a sanitarium near Chicago, where she reportedly grew increasingly difficult to manage despite having been confined under relatively lax conditions.[22] The following year, a court declared her sane and she moved to France for four years, returning to the United States in 1880 to live with her sister, Elizabeth Edwards, in her Springfield home two years before suffering a fatal stroke.

Though history indicates she was once a helpmate to her husband, accounts of Mary's volatile disposition, materialistic obsessions, and mental devolution – even if worsened by her numerous personal losses – have come to define her image as first lady, making her appear more of a liability than a leader in the White House.

ABOVE: An illustration of Abraham Lincoln's 1865 assassination committed by Confederate sympathizer John Wilkes Booth at Ford's Theatre in Washington.

ELIZA McCARDLE JOHNSON

(1810 – 76)

FIRST LADY: 15 APRIL 1865–4 MARCH 1869

One of history's most reclusive first ladies, Eliza Johnson entered the White House amid upheaval following President Abraham Lincoln's assassination, as her husband was tasked with taking the reins of the upended administration and leading the nation through the aftermath of the Civil War.

Eliza, unlike certain other first-ladies-to-be, did not have a childhood blessed with privilege. Born in Washington County, Tennessee, in 1810 to a father who worked as an innkeeper and a cobbler, Eliza and her mother were left impoverished when he died only 16 years later. In spite of the hardship, Eliza managed to obtain an education at Greeneville's Rhea Academy, and further propelled her learning as an avid reader.[1]

It was in that city that she met Andrew Johnson the year of her father's death. As legend has it, Andrew had just moved to town and was looking for directions.[2] Eliza was supposedly the first person he saw.[3] Little did she know she would be courted by a man destined to hold the nation's highest office. In 1827, they wed while both were still in their teenage years.

Eliza was notably more erudite than her new husband, who worked as a tailor – a marked difference from former presidents whose résumés were decorated with lawyering experience or military service. Historians emphasize that he did indeed know how to read and write; however, Eliza proved to be a mentor in his education, helping him to refine his literacy and teaching

him arithmetic. While she is not remembered as having been active in Washington, she played a key role in preparing Andrew for political life.

Though Andrew never attended school, Eliza persuaded him to join the Greeneville College Debating Society, which allowed him to hone his abilities as an orator.[4] Shortly after, he headed up a workingman's party and served as a city alderman before being elected mayor in 1834.[5]

Gradually, he made his way from local politics to the state legislature, eventually entering Washington as a congressman representing Tennessee in 1843. Ten years later, he would return to his state as its governor, move back to the capital city as a senator, then travel home once again to take up a military governorship to which he had been appointed by Lincoln during the war.

As Andrew ascended the ranks and became increasingly engaged in his career, Eliza, who had almost certainly not expected him to enter politics, took control of the family finances, all while looking after their two daughters and three sons with the help of a slave.

During the early 1850s, Eliza began showing symptoms of tuberculosis, an illness that would become persistent and debilitating throughout the remainder of her life. Even during Andrew's time as a senator, Eliza avoided Washington, believing she was better off attempting to recover in Tennessee.[6]

When Johnson assumed the presidency, having served as vice president for six weeks in 1865 when Lincoln was suddenly murdered, Eliza sequestered

herself, like other invalid or introverted first ladies, in a second-floor room and attended very few events.[7]

Rather than serving as the official White House hostess, Eliza effectively relinquished her position to daughter Martha Johnson Patterson, who humbly acknowledged upon assuming the role of hostess that tragedy is what led her family to its newfound power. "We are plain people, from the mountains of Tennessee, called here for a short time by a national calamity," she said.[8] "I trust too much will not be expected of us."[9]

Though Martha was unassuming in nature, *The Ladies' Home Journal* commended her, declaring, "It is doubtful if there is in America any other woman who has trod in so many paths of fame and fortune and personal grief combined."[10] Aside from routine hostessing duties, one of her first projects was restoring the condition of the White House, which was left "in a deplorable condition of dirt and general disorder, owing to its frequent, and often unavoidable ill-treatment during the war," according to the *Journal*.[11]

Eliza, so noticeably absent from her public role that she was described by one newspaper as "almost a myth,"[12] candidly declared to the press in her only known public statement, "My dears, I am an invalid."[13] However, speculation that she held no influence fails to give Eliza sufficient credit for her work behind the scenes. Being as active as her health permitted, she consumed a variety of newspapers, clipping items of interest and sharing them with Andrew.[14] She even assisted him in preparing his speeches.[15]

As her room was across from the president's office, Eliza was able to maintain close proximity to his discussions and cool his temper if needed, sometimes offering her thoughts or advice.[16]

In 1868, one year before the end of Andrew's presidency, Eliza continued to support her husband as impeachment proceedings were launched against him over his refusal to comply with an unconstitutional law mandating that he obtain congressional approval of any cabinet firings. Andrew, who had ousted Edwin Stanton, his secretary of war with whom he had a contentious relationship, had suddenly become the star of a month-long trial so popular that tickets were sold to members of the public who wished to watch the spectacle.[17]

Confident the charges against him would be dropped, Eliza and her family continued with the daily business of the White House, showing composure amid chaos. Aiming to keep Andrew's spirits high, Eliza brought him only good news before bed, holding off on sharing any bad press until dawn.[18]

William Henry Crook, Andrew's bodyguard, personally attested to Eliza's quiet strength in the White House, crediting her family's "undisturbed peacefulness" to "the deeply reverent spirit of Mrs. Johnson, who was absolutely convinced of her

husband's desire to do what was right, even though he might be mistaken."[19]

Upon notifying Eliza of her husband's acquittal, Crook recalled that despite her frailness, she stood up from her chair and simply responded, "I knew it."[20]

ABOVE: Portrait of Andrew Jackson.

RESTORATION OF THE WHITE HOUSE

As a busy hub during the Civil War, the White House had become very run down. The furnishings were infested with insects, the carpets filthy and the curtains ragged. The building was in no state to play host to formal receptions. Daughter Martha was tasked with organizing the renovation of the building, and her first decision on receiving $30,000 of funds from congress was to prioritize the appearance of the public rooms over the private quarters.

Martha's strategy was to restore and repair as far as possible, rather than spending on brand new furniture. Panelling and decorative elements were added to walls rather than expensive repapering, and the floors were cleaned and restored. Martha directed proceedings, supervising all of the staff involved in the restoration process, and the building was ready for guests by the autumn of 1866. [21]

Perhaps the most significant achievement made by Martha in this refurbishment was the rediscovery and framing of a series of portraits of past presidents. These can still be seen today in the Transverse Hall.

JULIA DENT GRANT

(1826–1902)

Following Abraham Lincoln's assassination, the end of the Civil War and Andrew Johnson's impeachment trial, America had been rocked by death, destruction, and political strife. But like a sigh of relief, the Gilded Age – an era of flourishing opportunity and economic prosperity – had finally arrived, and Julia Grant was its embodiment.

Born in 1826 on her family's St. Louis, Missouri plantation, White Haven, Julia became accustomed to a life of privilege and comfort from childhood. At age 18, she met Ulysses Grant, then a young Army lieutenant and West Point graduate, who paid a visit to Julia's home as her brother was one of his classmates.[1] During their courtship, Ulysses made it known that he opposed slavery, clashing with Julia's father over the matter and his pursuit of her.[2] It wasn't until Ulysses returned from the Mexican War that Julia's father allowed them to marry.[3]

Though it remains unclear to what extent, if any, Julia influenced her husband in the White House, she certainly held influence in their personal relationship. While away on the battlefield, Ulysses confessed to Julia in a missive that "absent or present I am more or less governed by what I think is your will."[4]

Not only Ulysses' companion in love, Julia was also his partner in the Civil War, travelling beside him as she was able while taking up shelter in tents, boarding houses, and commandeered homes.[5] And she wasn't simply along for the ride – Julia visited ill soldiers, fraternizing with officers, and thereby becoming privy to her husband's military strategy.[6] In her own way, she shared in the full experience, from its hardships to its glories.

Unlike the dejection felt by many of her predecessors, Julia was thrilled at her husband's election in 1868, later describing her time in the White House as a "garden spot of orchids."[7] As first lady, she embraced the Gilded Age in all of its opulence, hosting extravagant dinners where guests were treated to high-priced French wines and seemingly endless courses. Certain events famously served up to 29 dishes.[8]

Though Mary Lincoln's evident shopping addiction made her the target of scrutiny, Julia was dealt only muted criticism as part of the nation – despite an increasingly stark class divide – overlooked her purchases as a sign of the times. Among the elite, money was power and spending translated to status. As mass consumption became sport, Julia evaded backlash even when ordering 570 pieces of White House china in 1870.[9]

The first lady did not, however, take to politics the way she took to hostessing. In one instance, the first lady mistakenly came out both in support and opposition of a single piece of legislation.[10] As Julia recalled, she was out shopping when confronted by the bill's proponents and its detractors, who were aiming to get their message to the president.[11] Caught off guard and knowing nothing about the

> ## "Absent or present I am more or less governed by what I think is your will."
>
> - ULYSSES S. GRANT TO JULIA GRANT, CIRCA 1844

measure, Julia appeared to endorse both sides.[12]

Later approaching Ulysses and asking him to explain the proposal, she urged the president to issue a veto. However, she eventually conceded that "the President knew his duty quite well and would have fulfilled his duty in any case."[13]

At the conclusion of Ulysses' second term in 1877, Julia did not express the relief likely felt by many first ladies who had entered the position reluctantly. Instead, she was struck with disappointment at her

husband's decision not to seek a third term against her encouragement, declaring that she was "deeply injured" by his choice.[14]

Ultimately, unlike Abigail Adams or Sarah Polk, Julia's legacy was not defined by an eagerness to affect the course of politics. However, her efforts at entertaining in the White House breathed life into the position of first lady, which had previously been occupied by a number of women who were either unwilling or unable to seize the role's full potential.

OPPOSITE: The Grants at their family cottage in Wilton, New York, just nine miles from Saratoga Springs.

LOYALTY IN PRINT

Not until nearly a century later would the full scope of Julia's loyalty to her husband and his presidency be understood. After leaving the White House, days before his death, Ulysses completed a memoir that earned half a million dollars' worth of royalties.[15] Noticing the success of his book, Julia wrote her own, though she never found a willing publisher and her manuscript was left unprinted until 1975 – 73 years after her death – when it finally hit the shelves.[16] In several of its pages, she emerges as Ulysses' defender, chiefly regarding the so-called Black Friday gold scandal of 1869, during which two financiers – Jim Fisk and Jay Gould – attempted to corner the market in a scam for riches. The duo received help from Ulysses' brother-in-law and erroneously believed they also had the president's stamp of approval. When carried out, the plot went awry, causing the gold market to crash and leaving Ulysses' administration blighted. Yet in her account of the controversy, Julia painted her husband as an innocent and naive man who had no part in the con.[17] In fact, Julia wrote that Ulysses had even asked her to warn his sister in a letter of Fisk and Gould's deceptive ways so that her husband would keep his distance from the two.[18]

LUCY WARE WEBB HAYES

(1831–89)

FIRST LADY: 4 MARCH 1877–4 MARCH 1881

Credited with ushering in the era of the "New Woman" marked by emerging independence and self-governance, Lucy Hayes was the first presidential wife to enter the White House with a college degree and a major activist initiative: temperance.

Lucy grew up in Chillicothe, Ohio, with a strong belief in abstinence from alcohol instilled by her grandfather, Isaac Cook, a state legislator, judge, and influential force in Lucy's life following the death of her father in 1833 when she was just two years old. Those values shaped during childhood would one day come to define her first ladyship.

In 1844, Lucy's family moved to Delaware, where she attended Ohio Wesleyan Preparatory School followed by Wesleyan Female College in Cincinnati. She was a devout Methodist and both institutions awarded her merit points for honourable conduct, an early sign of the character for which she would be remembered in the White House.[1] She wasn't only principled, she was smart. And the president-to-be – a young lawyer and family acquaintance – took note.

In 1851, as their courtship was in full swing, Rutherford Hayes revealed glowing admiration for Lucy in his diary, professing his love and remarking on her intellect, which he described as "a quick spritely one, rather than a reflective profound one."[2]

"She sees at a glance what others study upon, but will not, perhaps study what she is unable to see at a flash," he wrote.[3] "She is a genuine woman, right from instinct and impulse rather than judgment and reflection."[4]

In 1852, Lucy and Rutherford married, and went on to have eight children. Five lived to maturity. However, Lucy did not adopt the mindset of a homemaker, and was ideologically aligned with certain attitudes of the growing feminist movement, once stating that women deserve better wages, even if they are left only to "violent methods" to achieve change.[5]

When the Civil War broke out in 1861 and Rutherford volunteered to enlist at Lucy's encouragement, being promoted from an infantry commander to a general,[6] she found a leadership role of her own. Travelling alongside her husband to his encampments and tending to the wounded and dying, she became known to soldiers as "Mother Lucy,"[7] and undoubtedly bore witness to the horrors wrought by battle.

In the aftermath of the war, Rutherford's distinguished service allowed him to enter the political arena. In 1865, he was elected to Congress, and in 1868, governor of Ohio.

In 1877, Rutherford assumed the presidency amid the fallout of the nation's most contentious election yet, which he won on a thin and disputed margin, inspiring the derisive nickname, "His Fraudulency."[8] The hostile atmosphere hanging over his entry into the White House would have been of no benefit to Lucy's reputation, but nonetheless, the press fawned over America's new first lady.

Describing Inauguration Day, *New York Independent* columnist Mary Clemmer remarked that she had "never seen such a face reign in the White House," calling Lucy "strong as she is fair."[9] The seriousness of her physical appearance – from her conservative hairstyle to her eyes, which Clemmer said gleamed with a "tender light," – embodied the age of the so-called new woman concerned with substantive matters and meaningful reform.[10]

Despite what she described as her "smiling and pleasant exterior,"[11] Lucy felt intensely loyal to her husband, and on at least one occasion expressed in stark terms her frustration with his critics: "I keep myself outwardly very quiet and calm, but inwardly there is a burning venom and wrath,"[12] she told Rutherford, indicating that she was more complex than her image in the press might have suggested.

While Lucy did not promote the feminist cause during her tenure, upon her exit from the White House in 1881, she had become one of the nation's most beloved first ladies, and, as her contemporary, Washington reporter Ben Perley Poore, put it, more influential than anyone since Dolley Mádison.[13]

OPPOSITE: Lucy Hayes pictured in the White House conservatory with her two youngest children, Scott and Fanny, and a friend, standing.

A RESTRAINED TENURE

Lucy was a staunch advocate for temperance in the White House, giving her tenure a gravity and discipline that was lacking from that of her predecessor, Julia Grant, who embraced the rampant consumerism of the Gilded Age. Though Rutherford would have been the one to implement the alcohol ban, the first lady's dedication to the cause was a driving factor, prompting critics to dub her "Lemonade Lucy."

When it came to material objects, Lucy showed the same restraint, saving clothing receipts as a testament to her thrifty purchases, and repurposing old furniture from the attic when Congress declined to appropriate funds to renovate the executive mansion.[14]

However, Lucy's principled stands did not result in activism on suffrage. The first lady, who had once defended the use of violence for the sake of fairer pay, did not support voting rights for women, and ultimately fell into a relatively traditional hostessing role. Nonetheless, she showed quiet strength and the humility of a humanitarian, once sewing a Civil War veteran's uniform at the White House when the man, who was to be photographed during his visit, realized it did not bear the proper insignia.[15]

LUCRETIA RUDOLPH GARFIELD

(1832–1918)

FIRST LADY: 4 MARCH 1881–19 SEPTEMBER 1881

Strong-minded, well educated and independent, Lucretia Garfield had all the makings of a powerful first lady. Instead, hers is a story of what might have been.

Born in Garrettsville, Ohio, in 1832, Lucretia crossed paths with James Garfield while studying at Western Reserve Eclectic Institute, known today as Hiram College. Though James soon transferred to Williams College in Massachusetts, he courted her from afar, having admittedly been drawn to her intellect.

"I have for a series of years been accquainted [sic] with Miss Lucretia Rudolph and have been for several months studying her nature & mind," he wrote in an 1853 diary entry.[1] Still, he harboured reservations as to "whether she has that warmth of feeling – that loving nature which I need to make me happy."[2]

Despite their many love letters rich with glowing admiration – a trove of which remains preserved to this day – James's initial doubts over their compatibility proved an omen of the strife that would eventually plague their union.

At their cores, Lucretia and James held stark differences in values, their relationship managing to stay afloat perhaps only because where he wasn't willing to compromise, she was willing to sacrifice.

While she did not support suffrage, like Sarah Polk and Lucy Hayes, certain of Lucretia's principles paralleled the feminist cause.[3] James, taking notice of that unnerving truth, wrote, "There are some of her notions concerning the relation between the sexes which, if I understand, I do not like."[4]

Just three months before they married in 1858, Lucretia acknowledged that she wasn't cut out to play second fiddle to her husband's ambitions. "My heart is not yet schooled to an entire submission to that destiny which will make me the wife of the one who marries me because an inexorable fate demands it," she wrote to James, adding that her "heart almost breaks with the cruel thought that our marriage is based upon the cold stern word *duty*."[5]

After their wedding, Lucretia lived as if she were single, maintaining her teaching career and earning money while tending to few household chores.[6]

James, who joined the state legislature in 1859 and later enlisted in the Civil War, was frequently away, so much so that Lucretia estimated that they spent a mere five months together within more than four years of marriage.[7] During that time, Lucretia willingly bent to fit her husband's definition of an ideal companion, writing to James in 1860 that she would "try harder than ever before to be the best little wife possible."[8] She told him, "You need not be afraid of my introducing one of those long talks – such a terror to you – ever again."[9]

Amid the turmoil, two of the couple's seven children died within months of each other, adding further to their troubles.

James was evidently no advocate for gender equality, but when he won the Republican presidential nomination in 1880, he sought Lucretia's blessing, writing to her, "if the results meet your approval, I shall be content."[10] The

19 APRIL 1832 // Born in Garrettsville, Ohio

1838–47 // Studies at Garrettsville Public Grammar School

1847–49 // Attends Geauga Seminary, Chester, Ohio. Studies Greek, Latin, algebra, science, geography, and music

1850–55 // Attends Western Reserve Eclectic Institute, Hiram, Ohio. Meets Greek teacher James Garfield

1858 // Marries Garfield at her parents' home in Hiram

1860 // Gives birth to Eliza, first of seven children, of whom five survived

1869 // The couple build a home together in Washington, D.C., so the family can be together year round

1880 // Garfield is nominated for Republican presidential candidate

1881 // The Garfields become president and first lady, but their tenure is cut short by Garfield's assassination only six months into his presidency

ABOVE: A portrait of James Garfield.

gesture was a small indication that he took into account her personal views. Lucretia gave James's campaign the green light, and the following year, she assumed her role as first lady.

Her tenure was largely unremarkable, though her diary indicates she had a toughness about her, and, like other first ladies, could defend her husband as his ally.

In one such instance, Lucretia recalled a visit from a journalist who questioned whether James was truly running his administration out of his own desires, or being influenced by then-Speaker of the House of Representatives James Blaine.[11] "I made her understand ... that the President knew not only the men around him but also knows what he is about," Lucretia wrote of her conversation with the reporter,[12] indicating that at times, she could be assertive.

When it came to overturning her predecessor's ban on alcohol in the White House, Lucretia refused to budge, even at the urging of a

temperance advocate, noting that "drinking wine at a respectable dinner was so small a factor in bringing about the intemperance of the country that I felt there was great inconsistency in giving it so much importance."[13]

Lucretia's strength faced one of its greatest tests when an assassin shot on her husband in July 1881, leaving him bedridden for months as she kept watch at his side.[14] Praising her stoicism, one newspaper called her "the bravest woman in the universe."[15] In September, he succumbed to his injuries.

Following James's death, Lucretia became the first presidential wife to attend her husband's memorial services, which women had previously avoided as the events were considered too emotionally overwhelming.

Receiving an outpouring of support from across the nation, Lucretia subsequently acquired substantial wealth, not through James's estate but $360,000 worth of contributions from the public and a $5,000 annual pension awarded by Congress.[16]

ELLEN LEWIS HERNDON ARTHUR

(1837–80)

Ellen Arthur never actually served as first lady, having died almost two years before her husband took office, but even in her absence, she wielded political influence over the president, as if to be an apparition in the White House.

Like others before her, Ellen came from an aristocratic Virginia family well-acquainted with Washington society, thanks to her father, a naval officer whose work required the family to move first to the capital then to New York where he was a steamship commander.[1] In both cities, Ellen became known as an accomplished singer, performing in the choir at historic St. John's Episcopal Church in Washington and the Mendelssohn Glee Club in New York.[2] It was there that she met young attorney Chester Arthur, and the two married in 1859. In a tragic turn of events, Ellen died of pneumonia in the winter of 1880.

Chester surely could not have foreseen his presidency, which transpired in the fall of 1881 amid national upheaval over the assassination of James Garfield. The new president, still in mourning over the loss of his wife, vowed never to allow a woman to take Ellen's place.

At first, Chester helmed a massive redecoration effort – a task that would have typically been organized by the first lady – selecting famed New York designer Louis Tiffany to renovate the executive mansion to the tune of more than $30,000 – a hefty bill for Congress in those days.[3] While Chester had taken it upon himself to spearhead the project in which the first lady would have traditionally been heavily involved, with nearly a full term to serve, Chester eventually invited his sister, Mary McElroy, to fill in as White House hostess.

Chester never granted the surrogate first lady the protocol rank her position would have held, refusing to do so in honour of Ellen's memory.[4] Nonetheless, Mary was well liked by the public, though she spent much of the year in Albany tending to her family, and the White House's social calendar was limited out of respect for the president's predecessor.[5]

Seemingly ever present in Chester's mind, Ellen's personal associations posthumously steered at least four presidential appointments.

William Arden Maury, who married Betty Herndon Maury, Ellen's first cousin, was made assistant attorney general.[6] Chester also lobbied for the hiring of Haughwout Howe, the son of Ellen's closest friend, as postmaster general.[7]

Two of the president's particularly controversial appointments were the selections of Captain Francis Ramsay, a relatively low-ranking officer, as superintendent of the naval academy, and Clayton McMichael as the district marshal of Washington, a position typically chosen by Senate leadership.[8] Both men had been Ellen's friends.[9]

The position of first lady was rather unexceptional during Chester's tenure, but much like the late Rachel Jackson, whose death husband Andrew Jackson blamed on the fury of his political foes, Ellen held power long after her passing.

FRANCES FOLSOM CLEVELAND

(1864-1947)

FIRST LADY: 2 JUNE 1886-4 MARCH 1889 / 4 MARCH 1893-4 MARCH 1897

To understand the development of the first ladyship as a nationally recognized role is to know Frances Cleveland, a woman who attained celebrity status thanks to a booming press and widespread public interest in her position.

Born in 1864 in Buffalo, New York, Frances had known Grover Cleveland since childhood, though he was nearly three decades her senior. When 11-year-old Frances's father died, Grover, who had been his law partner, looked after her. While not legally her guardian, Grover assumed such responsibilities.

Like two of her recent predecessors, Lucy Hayes and Lucretia Garfield, Frances was well educated, graduating from Wells College in nearby Aurora in 1885 with a bachelor's degree.

Grover, not yet married, assumed the presidency that year and enlisted sister Rose to take the reins as hostess-in-chief until his wedding to Frances in 1886 at a private White House ceremony – the first of its kind in the executive mansion. Frances's identity only became known to the country a week before the nuptials, whipping the media into a frenzy around history's youngest first lady.[1]

On their honeymoon, the newlyweds faced a barrage of invasive press, as reporters staked out the western Maryland cottage in which they were vacationing, surveying the couple with binoculars.[2] It was the dawn of so-called yellow journalism championed by iconic newspaperman Joseph Pulitzer, whose model of sensationalism sought to capture audiences with a good story, even if it meant barging into subjects' personal lives.

The coverage so irked Grover that in a letter to the *New York Evening Post* he decried the aggression of the press as "making American journalism contemptible."[3] But Frances didn't seem to mind the prying eyes, one writer noticing that "she could not bear with greater ease, tact, and graceful dignity the burden of social leadership which has fallen upon her."[4] After all, the same attention that Grover saw as a burden would come to solidify Frances's role as an institution unto itself; one worthy of massive public recognition.

While Frances undoubtedly could have used her stature as a source of political influence, she adopted a policy of non-engagement, receiving requests to support numerous reforms and declining to associate her name with such causes.[5] She was known to have endorsed temperance, though unlike the Hayes administration, she never imposed the policy in the White House, caring only about her own abstinence from alcohol.[6]

She could, however, be a political helpmate to her husband. During his re-election campaign in 1888, a woman wrote to the first lady questioning whether there was validity to rumours that Grover physically abused her. In a terse reply, Frances said she only wished that the husbands of all American women "may be as kind, attentive, considerate, and affectionate as mine."[7]

In spite of Benjamin Harrison's defeat of Grover, upon his departure from the White House, Frances confidently told the staff, "I want you to take good care of all the furniture and ornaments in the

PUBLIC PRESSURE

Frances grew so popular that her name and image were used to market an array of goods, from tobacco products and soaps to luggage and sewing machines, all without her consent.[9] On this, Frances pushed back. Upon seeing her likeness featured in an advertisement for face powder in *The Century Magazine*, she wrote to editor Richard Gilder, expressing her displeasure and requesting that it be scrapped.[10] The absence of advertising regulations became intensely problematic for the first lady, and spurred Congress to consider a legislative crackdown.[11] However, hampered by Grover's contentious relationship with lawmakers, no bill passed.[12]

In an attempt to escape the spotlight, Frances and Grover established Oak View, a second home roughly three miles away from the White House. Fed up with the press and concerned for his wife's safety, the president decided they would remain in the executive mansion only for the duration of its winter social season, then retreat to their alternate residence.[13] Such a concept had been debated since the government's inception, but the Clevelands were the first to make it work.[14]

house, and not let any of them get lost or broken, for I want to find everything just as it is now, when we come back again."[8] And indeed they did return, just four years later.

Grover's second term was plagued by devastating nationwide economic strife, though joy came with the birth of his second daughter, Esther, in the White House – another first for the executive mansion. Sadly, he wouldn't live to see much of her life, dying in 1908.

Frances remarried five years later, becoming the first presidential widow to take another husband.

OPPOSITE: The president and the first lady at their Princeton, New Jersey home in 1907, pictured with their four children, Esther, Francis Grover, Marion and Richard (left to right).

ABOVE LEFT: Coverage of the Clevelands' wedding in *Frank Leslie's Illustrated Newspaper*. The newlyweds found media attention inescapable following their nuptials.

CAROLINE LAVINIA SCOTT HARRISON

(1832-92)

FIRST LADY: 4 MARCH 1889-25 OCTOBER 1892

As the first ladyship grew into a nationally recognized role, bestowing upon its holders a near-celebrity status, Caroline Harrison could not escape criticism from detractors who questioned her concentration on domesticity in the White House, a focus that left her contributions to the empowerment of women outside the home largely overlooked.

Born in 1832 in Ohio, Caroline's belief in educational equality appears to have been a product of her father, a university professor who founded the state's Oxford Female Institute, where she eventually earned her college degree.

Caroline showed an aptitude for art as a skilled painter and she taught music in Kentucky. Her passions, however, took a backseat following her marriage to Benjamin Harrison in 1853, as the couple's focus shifted to the future president's career.[1]

During Benjamin's Senate term from 1881 to 1887, Caroline's opportunity to mingle with Washington society was hampered by perpetual illness, including respiratory ailments[2] that kept her from the city's winter social season.[3] However, at the start of her husband's presidency in 1889, Caroline settled into the White House, where she undertook a range of domestic duties, chief among which was her effort to modernize its interior. Her ambitious plan called for fountains and greenhouses, as well as the addition of an east and west wing to house offices and an art gallery,[4] neither of which would

be built until 1902, as Congress refused to allocate funds for the idea.

Scaling back, Caroline oversaw a list of more modest updates, including new flooring, furniture, private baths, kitchen renovations, and the installation of electric lighting.[5] Her attention to household tasks prompted contemporary Washington correspondent Frank Carpenter to proclaim her "the best housekeeper that [the] Pennsylvania Avenue mansion has yet known."[6]

Even the property's electrician-turned-chief usher, Ike Hoover, who holds the all-time record for most years served in the position, took notice, stating that although the Harrison administration had "accomplished nothing startling," Caroline made an "imprint everywhere around the White House."[7] That rang especially true when the first lady used her creative talents to design the china patterns – a combination of cornstalk and goldenrod.

As Hoover recalled, the refurbishment was so extensive that when Grover Cleveland returned with wife Frances for his second term, "they hardly recognized the house which they had left only four years before."[8]

But the very work that brought Caroline praise also triggered scrutiny. According to historian and curator emerita for political history at the National Museum of American History, Edith Mayo, rumours flew that Caroline was simply engaged in domestic chores rather than meaningful initiatives,

1 OCTOBER 1832 // Born in Oxford, Ohio

1848 // Meets Benjamin Harrison when her family moves to College Hill, Cincinnati

1852 // Graduates from Oxford Female Institute with a degree in music

1853 // The couple are married at Caroline's family home

1854 // Their first child, Russell, is born. Their second, Mary, follows in 1858.

1888 // Harrison is nominated as Republican presidential candidate

1890 // Founds the National Society of the Daughters of the American Revolution

1891 // Caroline oversees extensive updates to the White House, including the installation of electricity

1892 // Succumbs to tuberculosis and dies in the White House

ABOVE: A White House portrait of the first lady completed in 1894 by Daniel Huntington.

OPPOSITE: The first lady's bedroom, c. 1889–92.

Mrs. Harrison's Bedroom, President's Mansion, Washington, D.C.

which "was seen as very much beneath the dignity of a first lady."[9]

As Mayo states, Caroline "could not fathom why there was all this scorn and mocking in the press of what she was doing in the White House, but people didn't quite understand what she was trying to accomplish."[10]

Outside of her duties as first lady, Caroline pushed for co-education of women at Johns Hopkins Medical School upon its founding in 1890, through a lobbying effort helmed by leaders including Elizabeth Blackwell, the nation's first female doctor, and Louisa Catherine Adams, the granddaughter of the former first lady of the same name.[11]

As a condition of fundraising $100,000 for the institution's establishment, the women demanded that it commit to welcoming female students.[12] In the end, the bargain proved successful, marking a major step forward in educational equality.[13]

Further promoting heightened visibility for women, Caroline became the first president general of the Daughters of the American Revolution, an organization of women whose heritage traces back to those involved in the United States' fight for independence. While intended to honour the nation's history, the group's creation was spurred on by its male equivalent, the Sons of the American Revolution, which had voted to restrict women from joining.

Caroline's tenure as first lady was cut short in 1892 when she became ill with tuberculosis, which turned fatal just before the end of her husband's term.

Though much attention has been given to her domestically inclined agenda in the White House, the first lady's use of her position to advocate for the empowerment of women at large – an action certain of her predecessors declined to take – should not be overlooked.

IDA SAXTON McKINLEY

(1847–1907)

FIRST LADY: 4 MARCH 1897–14 SEPTEMBER 1901

Afflicted by perpetual illness, the loss of her only two children, and, eventually, the assassination of her husband, Ida McKinley faced a life marked by tragedy with stoicism and great strength.

Born in Canton, Ohio, in 1847, Ida's family, much like that of Caroline Harrison, believed in women's education, affording her the opportunity to spend ample time in the classroom. In 1868, she began working as a teller at her father's Stark County Bank, graduating to the position of manager – a highly unusual post for a woman at a time when professions such as teaching were far more common for women.

At the bank, Ida's all-male co-workers reacted with disapproval at her employment there, feeling it was a product of her "over-education."[1] Defending her work, she contended it was her father's wish that she pursue a means of self-support that didn't hinge upon marriage.[2]

That year, Ida met William McKinley, an army major-turned-lawyer, whom she married in 1871. Within months, their first daughter, Katherine, was born, followed by the birth of their second daughter, "Little Ida," in 1873. But suddenly, the family suffered a spate of losses all at once. Two weeks before Little Ida entered the world, Ida's mother died. About five months later, Little Ida died. Not long after, in 1875, so did Katherine.

Ida carried on, though she understandably lapsed into a depressive state, even taking refuge in Buddhism and the concept of reincarnation with the hopes of keeping Katherine's memory alive.[3] According to historian Carl Sferrazza Anthony, author of the first full-length biography of Ida McKinley, various firsthand accounts recall that she stared at young children in whom she suspected the soul of her lost child lived on.[4]

At some point within her immense grieving, Ida is believed to have struck her head, potentially triggering an onset of epilepsy.[5] Further complicating matters, she suffered a weak immune system and neurological damage that partially immobilized one leg.[6]

Ida received glowing praise for her enduring fortitude, being lauded as "an inspiration to all women" who "for one reason or another are hindered from playing a brilliant individual role in life" by *Harper's Bazaar* editor Elizabeth Jordan.[7]

Following William's election, Ida's health gradually worsened, but the first lady fulfilled her duties to the extent that she was physically capable, as the McKinleys adopted a business-as-usual approach to life in the White House.[8]

Ida did not champion any particular initiative but supported both the Salvation Army and Crittenden House, an organization that provided food, shelter, and employment training to jobless and homeless women.[9] She also famously took to knitting slippers, which she donated to charity group auctions rather than making public appearances.[10]

At White House dinners, William attempted to maintain a semblance of normalcy when it came to Ida's health, and was rumoured to have covered her face with a napkin in the event that she lapsed into a seizure while in the company of guests.[11]

Through her hardship, those who knew Ida remarked on her ability to muster a brave face. As biographer Thomas Beer wrote in his 1929 biography of Ohio Senator Mark Hanna, an ally of William, the first lady had "a certain bright intelligence and was sometimes witty enough to amuse" secretary of state John Hay.[12]

"I'm tremendously glad that I married a woman with a sense of humor," the president once said.[13]

In 1901, tragedy befell Ida once again when an anarchist Leon Czolgosz shot William while the president was at an event in Buffalo, New York. For eight days, he languished in bed, but in those moments, Ida again showed courage. According to a newspaper report published two days after the shooting, Ida "did not break down" when she learned of the gravity of her husband's condition.[14] "On the contrary, feeble as she is, grief seemed to lend her strength, and she felt she must bear up for his sake," the account read.[15]

THE INVALID MYTH

Though unjust portrayals of Ida as an invalid have stubbornly persisted throughout history, her health did not render her inactive. In fact, during her husband's 1896 presidential run, she participated in his front-porch campaign at the couple's Canton home in which they had lived as newlyweds.[18] The McKinleys were then residing in a separate home nearby, only returning to the old property part time when William staged his election effort.[19]

While there, Ida met with political figures, voters, and the press, which gave her a chance to dispel notions that she may have been constrained by her health.[20] "I always forget that I cannot walk until someone reminds me of it," she said at the time.[21] "My husband's right arm has so taken the place of my foot that I have never been deprived of any enjoyment in life because of my lameness."[22]

RIGHT: Ida McKinley was often in poor health, and held bouquets of flowers at political functions to avoid shaking hands with guests.

After William's death, Ida accompanied him back to Ohio, where he was buried,[16] though she was prevented from attending any public memorial services.[17]

Ida did not have the chance, nor, perhaps, the will of certain of her predecessors to become politically engaged and shoulder the full extent of the expectations that had come to be connected to the role of first lady. Instead, her legacy rests in her ability to demonstrate great character in times of enormous adversity.

"He is gone, and life to me is dark now."

– IDA SAXTON McKINLEY, 1901

(4) Mrs. McKinley in the Conservatory of the Executive Mansion, Washington.
Copyright 1900 by Underwood & Underwood.

EDITH KERMIT CAROW ROOSEVELT

(1861–1948)

FIRST LADY: 14 SEPTEMBER 1901–4 MARCH 1909

Edith Roosevelt's tenure signalled a turning point in the transformation of the first ladyship from a *de facto* title bestowed upon a presidential wife to an institutionalized role. Handling heightened press attention as well as the demands of her position, Edith set a precedent of delegating and hiring paid staff rather than shouldering the full burden.

Born in Norwich, Connecticut, in 1861, Edith had known the future president since childhood, having been friends with his sister, Corrine. Though he had spoken glowingly of Edith as the "most cultivated, best-read girl I know,"[1] Theodore initially married Alice Hathaway Lee, whom he had met through her cousin, one of his Harvard peers. Two days after giving birth to their first child in 1884, Alice died of Bright's disease — known today as nephritis, a condition in which the kidneys become inflamed. In a tragic coincidence, his mother died of typhoid fever the same day.

In 1886, Theodore, who had previously written as a 25-year-old widower that his life had "been lived out,"[2] rekindled his relationship with Edith. That year, the two married and went on to have five children, bringing their brood's total to six.

Overall, Edith hadn't supported her husband's pursuit of a political career, worried about the financial cost[3] – an understandable concern given that money would have been tight within such a large household. In 1900, she even objected to Theodore's decision to join the Republican ticket as William McKinley's vice-presidential candidate, but went on to receive more than she had bargained

for when her husband assumed the presidency after William's assassination the following year.

Albeit Edith was no champion of Theodore's Washington aspirations, when it came time to move to the White House, she jumped in with experience, having served as the first lady of New York during her husband's governorship.

As first lady of the nation, Edith shaped the role in accordance with its growing expectations, hiring the first social secretary, Isabella Hagner, who had previously worked for the family of William McKinley's secretary of war, Russell Alger. Isabella assisted Edith in hosting social events, including receptions and teas, and was once called "the chief factor at the White House" by Theodore's military aide, Archibald Butt.[4]

Edith also employed caterers to manage the cooking and serving of meals, in doing so further adding a managerial aspect to the first ladyship.

In one of her key initiatives, Edith oversaw the White House's massive renovation in 1902, collaborating with a renowned architectural company, McKim, Mead & White, to separate residential quarters from executive offices and refurbish and enlarge public rooms.[5] When Caroline Harrison had proposed a nearly identical effort in 1889, Congress rejected it. However, by the time Theodore took office, the U.S. was establishing itself as a world power, and lawmakers felt the president's home should reflect the change,[6] granting the nearly year-long project an appropriation of about half a million dollars.[7]

"The perfection of the invisible government."

- HISTORIAN OWEN WISTER ON EDITH ROOSEVELT

Behind the scenes, Edith exercised a subtle but steady influence over the president, so much so that she was dubbed by writer and historian Owen Wister "the perfection of the invisible government."[8] Privately, she monitored the press, clipped articles for Theodore, lobbied for the creation of the National Gallery of Art, and acted as a back-channel communicator with British diplomat Cecil Spring Rice and U.S. ambassador to England Whitelaw Reid during the Russo-Japanese War.[9]

By the time she left the White House in 1909, Archibald Butt attested that she had carried out her tenure "without making a mistake."[10]

RIGHT: Edith Roosevelt poses for a portrait, c. 1902.

OPPOSITE: President Theodore Roosevelt pictured with First Lady Edith, their sons Theodore III, Kermit, Archibald, and Quentin, and daughters Alice and Ethel.

MEDIA ATTENTION

As the White House and the presidency received intensified media attention, holding its first ever press briefings, Edith proved to be an adept publicist. Although she was notorious for being irked by reporters, Edith realized that getting out in front of the story was better than hiding from it altogether.

As a result, the first lady devised a proactive approach to the press that showed she could control her image, distributing posed family photographs to various publications such as *McClure's* and *Harper's Bazaar*, which in turn printed them.[11]

When it came to news coverage, the Roosevelt family had all the trappings of a good story. The White House was filled with various pets, including dogs, cats, and guinea pigs, and in the governor's mansion, a bear named Jonathan Edwards, which Theodore recalled "added zest to life in more ways than one."[12]

The Roosevelt children provided even more excitement, becoming known for their playful antics, such as a time when nine-year-old Quentin, who had just bought snakes at a local pet shop, proceeded to drop them in his father's lap while he was meeting with attorney general Charles Bonaparte.[13]

HELEN HERRON TAFT

(1861–1943)

Throughout the nation's history of first ladies, it is unlikely that any has been as deserving of credit for her husband's rise to the presidency as Helen Taft, who, through sheer force of will, ensured that he rose to the highest office despite his lack of desire to assume the role.

Helen was born in 1861 in Cincinnati, Ohio, the city William Taft too called home. While their families had long associated, the two did not meet directly until a bobsledding party in 1879.

In 1883, Helen, who declared that it was high time she and her friends "became serious-minded" and occupy themselves with something "more satisfying than dancing and amateur theatricals," began teaching for two years, then headed up a "salon" for highbrow social gatherings. The purpose, she wrote in her 1914 memoir, was to create an invitation-only space for "brilliant discussion of topics intellectual and economic."[1]

Helen, who must have glimpsed William's potential early on, welcomed him to attend, recalling that the two "fought it out" with "high feeling and enthusiasm" while sparring over local politics at their meetings.[2]

For the future first lady, education was of paramount importance, and essential in fostering gender equality. "My idea about higher culture for women is that it makes them great in intellect and soul, develops the lofty conception of womanhood; not that it makes them a poor imitation of man," she once said.[3]

William, embarking on a law career, took note of Helen's intelligence, complemented by her sheer ambition. In 1885, during their courtship, he wrote to his father, "Her eagerness for knowledge of all kinds puts me to shame. Her capacity for work is just wonderful."[4]

The following year, the couple married, and William quickly learned that his new wife's ambition wasn't just personal. She had visions for his future as well, and would accept nothing short of greatness.

William advanced through a series of legal appointments, becoming a Cincinnati superior court judge in 1887, then U.S. solicitor general in 1890 and two years later, judge of the U.S. Circuit Court of Appeals for the Sixth Circuit. However, his growing success did cause Helen to fret that she would fade into the background, playing a one-dimensional role as his wife.[5]

But after the Spanish-American War, to her excitement, opportunity came knocking when President William McKinley asked her husband to travel to the Philippines, which had just been ceded to the U.S. While there, he would serve as the president of a commission tasked with establishing a civil government. In many aspects, it functioned as a trial run for his eventual rise to the White House, and Helen knew it was a chance for him to show he was capable.[6]

"I wasn't sure what it meant, but I knew instantly that I didn't want to miss a big and novel experience," she said.[7]

Just as the assignment gave William a taste of presidential duties, it also placed Helen in an

> "It seems to me that, geographically and logically, Washington should be the representative social city of the land."
>
> – HELEN HERRON TAFT, 1909

experimental first ladyship of sorts in which she became invested in ending infant mortality on the islands, promoting health care, and improving nutrition.[8] Her initiative was eventually organized into the so-called Drop of Milk charity, which provided sterilized milk to families.[9]

In 1906, well after the Tafts had returned stateside, Helen grew increasingly concerned that William might be tapped for a lifetime supreme court appointment, which would foil her plan to see him elected president – a prospect that was already gaining public support.[10]

Taking matters into her own hands, Helen met with President Theodore Roosevelt, who subsequently wrote to William that while he had thought William had his sights set on the bench, "a half-hour's talk with your dear wife" – in addition to a letter from William – indicated that he was mistaken as to what the future president desired.[11]

William, who reluctantly became the Republican nominee, called his campaign "one of the most uncomfortable four months of my life."[12] Nonetheless, in 1909, he and Helen entered the White House.

In a remarkably cruel twist of fate, two months after his inauguration, Helen suffered a severe stroke, temporarily rendering her unable to speak. Eventually, she regained her abilities through therapy, though her speech was permanently altered.[13]

Despite the health challenges, Helen remained fairly active in her role, famously arranging the planting of thousands of cherry trees around Washington, D.C.'s Tidal Basin, which remain one of the city's major attractions today.[14]

Helen – much like her visions for her husband – saw the city's potential for greatness, and dedicated herself to making the White House the social hub of the nation. "It seems to me that, geographically and logically, Washington should be the representative social city of the land," she told the *New York American*, adding that she hoped "one day to see it the recognized social center of the United States."[15]

Like Edith Roosevelt, Helen too had a social secretary during the first part of her tenure,[16] an indication that a precedent for paid staff for first ladies had been set. Helen also oversaw the family

finances by adopting a strict budget, managing to accumulate a $100,000 nest egg in their bank account by the time William left office in 1913.[17] According to Washington scribe Edna Colman, who chronicled the lives of the presidents in her 1927 book, *White House Gossip*, "All her life she had been a careful manager, a fact to which her husband often referred with pride."[18]

When it came to politics, just as she spurred William's decision to pursue the presidency, she influenced his decisions in the White House. The first lady took the liberty of offering advice on various appointments, including that of an ambassador to France whom she had recalled, still irked over an instance on her honeymoon during which he had slighted her more than two decades prior.[19] It may have been trivial, but it proved she carried clout.

William, to Helen's disappointment, failed to win a second term, but without their partnership, it is unlikely he would have served the first. That, in large part, remains Helen's legacy.

As a *Ladies Home Journal* article told readers following his election, "Had it not been for his wife, Mr. Taft would never have entered the presidential race."[20]

ABOVE: Helen Taft boards a presidential automobile as she sets out on a shopping trip.

ELLEN AXSON WILSON

(1860–1914)

For a first lady who declared just before entering the White House that she had no interest in the role she was about to assume, Ellen Wilson made a sizable impact in her year-long tenure, which was cut short by illness.

Born in 1860 in Savannah, Georgia, Ellen moved around as a child of the Civil War era as her family attempted to steer clear of war zones, eventually settling in the small town of Rome where she met Woodrow, a young attorney, in 1883.

By certain accounts, Ellen was strong-minded and independent, so much so that one observer speculated she would inevitably marry "an insignificant man" because "bright people rarely ever married people who were their equal in intellect."[1] Though the future first lady went on to marry perhaps the country's most significant man of all, she once cautioned a friend to "use all your faculties before beginning to yield to a man's fascinations."[2]

She followed her own advice, even if only for a short time. During her courtship with Woodrow, Ellen, who had budding artistic talents, made clear that she intended to devote time to her passion, and spent a year at the Art Students League of New York. Unlike most other institutions of higher education at the time, the school accepted both men and women, though they attended classes at varying times.[3]

In 1885, shortly after the end of Ellen's time in New York, she and Woodrow married and went on to have three daughters.

Ellen's attention soon turned to her husband's career, as he had become the president of Princeton University after shifting his focus from law to academia. His position placed Ellen in a public role in which she took on the duties of a social hostess and manager of their household, overseeing entertainment, renovations, and garden maintenance.[4]

In 1910, when Woodrow earned the Democratic nomination for governor of New Jersey and scored a landslide victory, Ellen had her first brush with the national media as the Wilsons were profiled in women's magazine *The Delineato.*[5]

As support mounted for Woodrow to launch a presidential bid, Ellen worked in an informal capacity as his campaign manager, monitoring news coverage and flagging items of importance. As biographer Ray Stannard Baker later wrote, Ellen "followed indefatigably, as she had been doing for years, everything that she thought would assist her husband… and clipped out everything related to the campaign."[6]

In many regards, she was well acquainted with the expectations of a first lady by the time she took on the role in 1913. However, she purported to have no desire for the job. Before moving into the White House, Ellen wrote to President William Taft, "I am naturally the most unambitious of women and life in the White House has no attractions for me! Quite the contrary in fact!"[7]

Despite that claim, Ellen backed the controversial Slum Clearance Bill to tear down Washington's dilapidated alleyway dwellings. After touring the predominantly black settlements and bearing

15 MAY 1860 // Born in Savannah, Georgia

1883 // Meets Woodrow Wilson in Rome, Georgia, when he is visiting family

c.1883–85 // Studies at the Art Students League of New York, winning a medal for a painting at the Paris International Exposition

1885 // Marries Wilson at her grandparents' home in Savannah

1886–89 // The Wilsons have three daughters: Margaret, Jessie and Eleanor

1902 // Wilson becomes president of Princeton University, and Ellen takes up her social and hosting responsibilities, while continuing to pursue her art

1912 // Moves to the White House when Wilson is elected president

1914 // Dies of Bright's disease and is buried in Rome, Georgia

witness to extreme poverty, the first lady made herself a proponent of the policy to replace the shanty houses with parks. The initiative has been depicted throughout history as a product of Ellen's concern for social advocacy, but critics have scrutinized the plan as having carried an air of racism.[8] According to John Cooper, historian and professor emeritus at the University of Wisconsin, Ellen's idea was, in part, "to beautify Washington, not just to be helpful."[9]

The first lady rallied enthusiasm for the bill by designating a White House car for tours of the slums, routinely accompanying lawmakers on the ride.[10] Her involvement had become so widely noticed that the proposal was referred to as "Mrs. Wilson's Bill," and she was listed as a member of the congressional committee that oversaw its introduction.[11]

Seventeen months into her tenure, while pushing for action on the measure, Ellen was bedridden with Bright's disease – otherwise known as kidney inflammation – and in her last moments, stated that she would "be happier if I knew the alley bill had passed."[12] On the final day of her life, the Senate passed an amended version of the bill. The House subsequently followed suit, though because of the outbreak of World War I, it was never implemented.

Ellen's stay in the White House, though brief, set a precedent for first ladies looking not just to embrace a cause, but also to cement it with legislative action.

OPPOSITE: The first lady and the president, both seated in two armchairs on the left and right, surrounded by family.

EDITH BOLLING GALT WILSON

(1872–1961)

FIRST LADY: 18 DECEMBER 1915–4 MARCH 1921

More than any other first lady throughout history, Edith Wilson's tenure is the closest any woman has come to serving in a presidential capacity. However, the opportunity was born out of national crisis.

Edith, a widow of her first marriage, was introduced to Woodrow Wilson shortly after Ellen Wilson's death. The couple became close within a relatively brief period, allegedly sparking concerns among Democratic Party leaders that an impending wedding could alienate voters from backing the president for a second term.[1] Nonetheless, Woodrow and Edith married in 1915, little more than a year following Ellen's passing, placing a new first lady in the White House.

After the war came to a close, Woodrow set out on a speaking tour in 1919 to promote the ratification of his peace agreement – the Treaty of Versailles – and drum up support for U.S. entry into the League of Nations – neither of which ultimately came to fruition.

Days after returning,[2] Woodrow had a stroke, sending his health into severe decline. Rather than announce to the nation what had occurred, the White House went silent, leaving room for speculation and rumours. Publicly, the first lady declined to provide any statement on her husband's condition, agreeing with his inner circle that no word would get out.[3]

As Woodrow recovered, Edith put on a brave face, revealing in her memoir years later that despite her stoicism, "something had broken inside me," forcing

her "to wear a mask – not only to the public but to the one I loved best in the world; for he must never know how ill he was, and I must carry on."[4]

Meanwhile, both Democrats and Republicans confronted vice president Thomas Marshall, urging him to assume Woodrow's duties as they fretted his death was imminent.[5] Ellen, now both guardian and gatekeeper, found herself fighting off the naysayers to the detriment of the nation, her critics would argue.

As Colman writes, the first lady "busied herself with the job of keeping her husband alive and of getting him well enough to handle the reins of government himself, before they were tugged out of his limp hand by governmental action."[6]

Edith claimed in her memoir that upon asking Woodrow's doctor, Francis Decrum, whether the president should step down, he warned that his resignation "would have a bad effect on the country, and a serious effect on our patient."[7] She even went so far as to assert that Decrum instructed her to take the reins, purportedly stating, "Have everything come to you; weigh the importance of each matter, and see if it is possible by consultations with the respective heads of the Departments to solve them without the guidance of your husband."[8]

According to historian John Cooper's 2001 biography of Woodrow, "It is extremely doubtful that Decrum or any responsible physician" would have pushed for the president to remain in the White House.[9] "At the time, it was far more likely that she grasped at straws that the physicians held out," Cooper wrote.[10] "Those included Wilson's

undiminished intellectual capacity, uncertainty about the extent and permanency of the stroke's effects, and the likelihood of some improvement."[11]

But Edith pressed on, she said, and "studied every paper, sent from the different Secretaries or Senators, and tried to digest and present in tabloid form the things that, despite my vigilance, had to go to the President."[12] Though she acknowledged she did not make decisions on public affairs, she filtered what issues her husband saw, and what was held from his view.[13]

In 1921, having only made a partial recovery, Woodrow did not seek a third term, and died three years later.

Edith's actions as first lady, while largely a study in how not to handle a presidential crisis, ultimately placed her nearer to the nation's highest office than most women in history.

OPPOSITE: Edith Wilson, Woodrow Wilson and his daughter, Margaret, from his previous marriage, at the University of Louvain with the king and queen of Belgium.
RIGHT: The first lady and the president attend a ball game.

THE WHITE HOUSE DURING WORLD WAR I

As Washington scribe Edna Colman states, Edith "had no desire for publicity or for doing spectacular things either to promote the popularity of her husband or herself." The entry of the U.S. into World War I less than two years later prompted her to use "every personal effort to promote and inspire many of the different phases of war work that the participation of the United States demanded."[14]

Such effort included shuttering the executive mansion to visitors and employing a flock of 20 sheep to graze the lawns rather than paying a labourer, all while producing a sizable wool crop that was auctioned off for the Red Cross, with sometimes hefty bidding prices for the coveted material.[15] Edith also chaired the organization's Women's Volunteer Aid Committee of its Washington branch, which helped to supply military hospitals and operate canteens for troops.[16] Within the White House, worn rugs and discoloured wall coverings signalled that renovations were largely overlooked as Woodrow's administration pinched every penny.[17]

FLORENCE KLING HARDING

(1860–1924)

Florence Harding set a new record as the oldest first lady at the time to enter the White House, but she nonetheless projected a vibrant and energetic image, at the same time proving to be a shrewd manager of the media capable of masking the gravity of her declining health and tamping down her husband's rumoured affairs.

Florence met Warren Harding after divorcing her first husband, Henry DeWolfe, who was a member of her Ohio social group, the so-called rough set, which was known for taking part in roller-skating, among other sports.[1] Henry, who developed the reputation of a hard-drinking playboy, left Florence and their son before the child had turned two.[2]

An avid pianist who had studied at the Cincinnati Conservatory, Florence went on to teach piano classes in her Marion hometown, one of her students being Warren's sister. At the time, Warren was the publisher of a local newspaper, the *Marion Star,* and it wasn't long before the couple met.

In 1891, against her father's objections, Florence married Warren and became the manager of the *Star.* Her responsibilities included launching a circulation department, overseeing business accounts, assigning stories, and hiring the state's first female reporter, Jane Dixon.[3] As modern biographer Betty Caroli writes, she "devoted herself to Warren's career as though her own reputation were at stake."[4]

That same energy was brought to Warren's campaign. As he rose from state senator to lieutenant governor in the U.S. Senate, it became evident to one observer in Washington that Florence harboured a "ruthless ambition to become First Lady," having "constantly worked and made Warren work toward that end."[5]

However, she initially appeared reluctant to support his bid for the presidency, concerned about mumblings over his alleged infidelity and a reported affair with a far younger woman, Nan Britton, who eventually delivered her account in a tell-all book. Faced with the risk that a campaign could dredge up her husband's unsavoury private life, this was almost certainly no incentive for Florence to jump in as his political helpmate or aid.

To make matters worse, Florence was met with further uncertainty in 1920 when she enlisted clairvoyant Marcia Champney to provide insight about the future.[6] Marcia speculated that Warren was engaged in "many clandestine love affairs," and predicted that he would be elected president but then die a "sudden, violent or peculiar death."[7]

Shaken by the message, Florence cried: "If my husband is elected I can see but one word hanging over his head, 'Tragedy! Tragedy!'"[8]

As John Dean, White House counsel during the Nixon administration, later wrote, it is unlikely that Florence pushed her husband into the race, but once Warren entered, she didn't let him out.[9]

During the Indiana primary, as Warren was losing ground, he called campaign manager Harry Daugherty to inform him that he was ready to drop out and scale his focus back to the Senate.[10]

ABOVE: The first lady pictured using a movie camera on the White House lawn.

An evidently incensed Florence then snapped at Warren, grabbed the phone, and declared, "We're in this fight until hell freezes over."[11] She may not have wanted Warren to put his hat in the ring, but she wasn't a quitter.

When it came to the press, Florence again became an asset to her husband's campaign, advising him on how to best handle claims that he had black ancestry. In the context of the racism embedded in the early twentieth century, such stories were intended to hurt his image, and were sparked by his family's past aid to escaped slaves travelling the underground railroad.[12] Though the allegations would ultimately be debunked through DNA nearly a century later,[13] Florence decided Warren would not deign to address them, and no statement was made on the matter.[14]

Despite the potentially damaging rumours and Warren nearly having ended his campaign, he was elected by a landslide against Democratic Ohio governor James Cox. Taking credit for the victory,

Florence eventually asserted, "I know what's best for the President. I put him in the White House."[15]

As first lady, Florence's media strategy became essential to her tenure, and she was able to harness the power of the press to her benefit. Hobnobbing with reporters became routine, allowing Florence to foster a friendly relationship with the media. That was especially evident when she invited the Women's National Press Club on the presidential yacht, where she slapped the organization's president, Cora Rigby, on the back and said, "Well, here we are, all girls together."[16]

Florence, who was now 61 years old and had taken on the nickname of "Duchess," posed for photos occasionally used on movie-theatre newsreels and used cosmetics freely.[17]

Just as she knew when to welcome press attention, she knew when to keep journalists at bay. In 1923, on the mend from a near-fatal attack of nephritis, Florence welcomed female reporters to the White House, where she offered them an interview while wearing a velvet negligee and disclosing her illness in such depth that it "revolted" one person

"If my husband is elected I can see but one word hanging over his head, 'Tragedy! Tragedy!'"

– FLORENCE KLING HARDING, 1920

present.[18] However, initially, the ailment had not been reported for weeks and few details were available.[19]

In this way, Florence lived a private and public-facing life. That capacity to shift between worlds also served her well in handling the Prohibition Era. While she maintained that she abstained from alcohol in accordance with the law, Florence mixed drinks for the president and his associates.

Just as she had been largely quiet about the condition of her own health, information about the seriousness of her husband's health was not made public either, his death in 1923 shocking the nation.

Though officials said the cause was a stroke, certain doctors suspect it was a heart attack.[20]

Following Warren's death, Florence, in an apparent attempt to safeguard what was left of her husband's image, destroyed the majority of their private papers that may have revealed his affairs and the rampant corruption that plagued his administration.

BELOW: The first lady stands with the Girl Scouts outside the White House in 1922.

GRACE ANNA GOODHUE COOLIDGE

(1879–1957)

An accidental first lady who rose to the position through President Warren Harding's death, Grace Coolidge surpassed many of her predecessors in popularity.

Born in 1879 in Burlington, Vermont, Grace became the first first lady to complete a traditional four-year college education at the University of Vermont.[1] Following her graduation in 1902, she enrolled in a teacher-training program at the Clarke School for the Deaf in Northampton, Massachusetts. A young lawyer named Calvin Coolidge happened to be her neighbour. In 1905, Grace and Calvin married.

Before long Calvin climbed the ranks from local political posts to becoming the city's mayor, then state senator, lieutenant governor, then governor. Meanwhile, Grace cared for their two children. However, when Calvin became vice president, she was brought into the spotlight, relocating to Washington and overshadowing then-first lady Florence Harding, who was older and tended to pale in comparison with Grace's exuberance.[2]

Calvin was notoriously aloof, whereas Grace was prone to taking on the role of charmer, her personality serving as an antidote to his painfully sober moods. Unlike her husband, Grace admittedly didn't know much about politics, but she knew about people. When she became first lady in 1923, one critic – described by a *New Yorker* writer as an "old pelican with sugar-coated malice oozing from every pore" – questioned whether she could bear the weight of the job's social obligations.[3]

Grace responded with a smile.[4] "It's going to be glorious for me," she said.[5] I'm just thrilled to death. I just love it. We never could entertain before. We didn't have the money. Even the vice presidency didn't give us the position. Things will be different now."[6]

Not until the posthumous publication of her autobiography would it become evident just how much she sacrificed in the role. "This was I and yet not I, this was the wife of the President of the United States and she took precedence over me; my personal likes and dislikes must be subordinated to the consideration of those things which were required of her," Grace wrote, making clear that though she fulfilled every traditional expectation of a first lady, she had suppressed a part of herself to play that role.[7]

Calvin had discouraged Grace from attracting too much attention, wagging his finger when she enlisted a horseback-riding instructor to give her daily lessons.[8] Washington papers wasted no time publicizing the event, prompting Calvin to tell her, "I think you will find that you will get along at this job fully as well if you do not try anything new."[9] The mandate appeared to inhibit Grace's first ladyship, but she was successful in advocating for the disabled, harkening back to her days at the Clarke School. During her tenure in the White House, she raised $2 million for the institution, convincing Calvin to offer his support as he recruited wealthy friends to donate.[10] Helen Keller, a famed disability rights advocate who was both blind and deaf, was a known guest at the executive mansion – a testament to the impact of Grace's initiative.[11]

As her biographer, Ishbel Ross, said, "From her first day as mistress of the White House she presented a picture of dignity and warmth."[12]

LOU HENRY HOOVER

(1874–1944)

Well educated and well versed in public speaking, Lou Henry Hoover set a precedent for first ladies seeking to champion causes of their own in the White House, a tradition that would eventually be solidified as an expectation of those filling the role.

Lou was born in 1874 in Waterloo, Iowa, to parents who encouraged her enthusiasm for athletics and the outdoors,[1] a passion which would eventually lead her to graduate from Stanford University with a geology degree in 1898. She was the first woman in the U.S. to earn a degree in that field at the institution. It was there that she met Herbert Hoover, a mining engineer with whom she bonded over their common Iowa origins. In 1899, they married.

Herbert's work required him to travel to China where he was tasked with evaluating the conditions of the country's mines and recommending improvements, so the day after their wedding, the couple set sail and settled in the northern port city of Tientsin, now known as Tianjin.

Little did they know, the anti-imperialist Boxer Rebellion would break out the following year, placing the Hoovers under siege. Lou took the crisis in her stride. According to historian Annette Dunlap, Lou was at home one day when gunfire rang out, sending a bullet straight through her front door.[2] Rather than panic, "she pulled out a deck of cards and started playing solitaire and didn't even miss a beat," Dunlap said.[3] When Lou and Herbert were barricaded in the city, Lou took to first aid, helping to care for the injured.[4]

Despite the turbulence, life abroad afforded Lou the opportunity to learn Chinese, adding to several other foreign languages in which she was already fluent, including Latin. Her knowledge was of great assistance to Herbert, for whom she translated *De Re Metallica*, a 1565 Latin mining manual, into English.

In 1900, the Hoovers made London their home as Henry worked for British mining firm Bewick, Moreing and Company. In 1914, when World War I broke out in Europe, Lou again jumped into action as she had in China, organizing relief efforts as Herbert led the Commission for Relief in Belgium to bring food to those stranded in the war zone. With Lou's help in rallying support, the organization raised nearly $600,000 from California, where she had family ties.[5] She became further active, as a national president of the Girl Scouts and the head of the Women's Division of National Amateur Athletic Federation.

Herbert, who had accepted the post of U.S. food administrator, then director general of the American Relief Administration addressing starvation in Europe, had drawn attention as a potential presidential candidate. After serving as secretary of commerce under the Harding and Coolidge administrations, Herbert launched a successful White House bid in 1928 as the Republican nominee.

Shortly after his inauguration, an address Lou delivered to the Daughters of the American Revolution was carried on radio – the first time a first lady had ever been heard on the airwaves. She went

29 MARCH 1874 // Born in Waterloo, Iowa

1898 // First woman to graduate with a BA in Geology from Stanford University – meets Herbert Hoover at Stanford

1899 // The couple marry at Lou's parents' home in Monterey, California

1899–1900 // Move to China, where Lou learns Mandarin – she is still the only first lady to speak an Asian language – moving to London when the Boxer Rebellion breaks out

1912 // Translates and publishes English-language edition of Agricola's *De Re Metallica*

1922–25 // Serves as national president of Girl Scouts of the U.S.

1929 // Moves into White House as first lady, serving until 1933

1944 // Dies at home in New York City

on to make numerous additional radio speeches, promoting volunteerism and public service, and ushering in a new era of visibility for presidential spouses that rose above attention to clothing and china pattern choices.

Lou knew how to use the press, though her interaction with media, for the most part, ended with radio. The first lady harboured a distrust of reporters, fuelled by the criticism with which she was met by southern newspapers after inviting the wife of Oscar DePriest, a black Chicago congressman, to tea at the White House.

As biographer Ishbel Ross recalled, Lou "was a tactful hostess but a problem for the press."[6]

"Mrs. Hoover figured little in the news except in connection with her Girl Scout activities, and on the few occasions that group interviews were arranged,

ABOVE: Lou Hoover presents awards to Girl Scouts Lucille Weber and Judith Steel.

the reporters were primed on the questions they might ask and were specifically warned against branching out in any direction except scouting," Ross wrote.[7]

In 1932, just weeks after her husband lost his re-election bid to Franklin Roosevelt, Lou delivered a radio speech on behalf of the National Women's Committee of the Welfare and Relief Mobilization, which sought to address the plight of the unemployed struggling to stay afloat in the Great Depression.

The speech, titled "The Woman's Place in the Present Emergency," urged women to consider it their "duty and privilege to help in every way possible those who are not as well off."[8]

Within her one-term tenure as first lady, Lou managed to campaign for a handful of charitable initiatives, taking her message nationwide in an effort to influence action, and setting the stage for her successors to become change-makers in their own right.

ABOVE: The president and first lady stand to attention in 1928.

ANNA ELEANOR ROOSEVELT

(1884–1962)

FIRST LADY: 4 MARCH 1933–12 APRIL 1945

Eleanor Roosevelt was the longest-serving first lady by virtue of her husband's unprecedented four successful bids for the White House in 1932, 1936, 1940, and 1944. Her tenure encompassed the Great Depression and World War II. During her reign, she redefined the first ladyship, pursuing an agenda that ranged from domestic social issues to global concerns. She was fiercely independent, outspoken, on occasion controversial, and sometimes at odds with the president. She was a woman who did not accept a subordinate role.

Born Anna Eleanor Roosevelt in 1884 to an aristocratic New York City family, she was nicknamed "Granny" by her socialite mother, Anna Hall, a celebrated beauty, who thought Eleanor plain in appearance and overly serious for a child. When Eleanor was six years old, Anna died, followed two years later by her father Elliott Roosevelt – a younger brother of former president Theodore Roosevelt. Eleanor and her siblings then went to live with their maternal grandmother.

As she matured, Eleanor shunned life as a debutante made to mingle with New York society, opting instead to become active in public service as a teacher for the Junior League for the Promotion of Settlement Movements, which addressed socioeconomic struggles borne by urban and immigrant Americans as a result of rapid industrialization. In this role, Eleanor taught calisthenics and dance to immigrant children at the city's College Settlement on Rivington Street, and bore witness to extreme poverty.

In 1903, she became an investigator for The Consumers' League, a reform organization advocating for sweatshop workers living and labouring in dangerous, unsanitary conditions. It was during this time that Eleanor became engaged to her distant cousin, Franklin Delano Roosevelt, a Harvard University graduate. In 1905, the two married, and went on to have six children, one of whom died in infancy.

For a brief time, Eleanor transitioned out of public service and focused heavily on her children, having been persuaded by her mother-in-law Sara Roosevelt – who would become a domineering figure in the couple's life – that she risked spreading germs at home through her work in the settlement houses.[1]

As Allida Black, founding editor of *The Eleanor Roosevelt Papers*, writes in her biography of the future first lady, "For most of her early life," she "lived in someone else's shadow."[2] But in 1910 when Franklin won a New York State Senate seat, and asked Eleanor to establish a second home in Albany,[3] she was out from under the critical gaze of her mother-in-law. "For the first time I was going to live on my own," Eleanor wrote more than two decades later. "I was beginning to realize that something within me craved to be an individual."[4]

When Franklin was appointed assistant secretary of the Navy under President Woodrow Wilson's administration, Eleanor followed him to Washington, where she made social calls and either hosted or attended various functions, dutifully cultivating contacts to further Franklin's career.[5]

11 OCTOBER 1884 // Born in New York City to parents Elliott and Anna Roosevelt, and niece of former president, Theodore Roosevelt

1894 // Elliott dies, leaving Eleanor an orphan. Her mother, Anna, died in 1892

1899 // Goes to study at Allenswood School, near London, England

17 MARCH 1905 // Marries FDR in New York

1910 // Having given birth to four children in five years, moves with family to Albany on FDR's election to the state senate

1917 // During World War I, volunteers with the Red Cross and works for the Navy-Marine Corps Relief Society

1922 // Becomes an active member of the Women's Trade Union League, campaigning for workers' rights

1927 // Establishes Val-Kill Industries, a small factory that would provide additional income to farming families in New York State

1932 // FDR elected president of the U. S.

1935 // Begins writing her daily newspaper column (a first for a first lady), which she would write until 1962

1941 // During World War II, co-chaired the Office of Civilian Defense and visits troops

1945 // Death of FDR. Eleanor is appointed the US Delegate to the UN, and served as US Representative to the UN Commission on Human Rights 1946–53

1948 // Addresses NAACP annual convention from steps of Lincoln Memorial

1961 // Appointed chair to the Commission on the Status of Women by JFK

7 NOVEMBER 1962 // Dies from complications due to tuberculosis

When the U.S. entered World War I, Eleanor became a Red Cross volunteer, supervising knitting operations and opening a canteen for soldiers travelling through Washington's Union Station.[6] Working from dawn to dusk, Eleanor was relentless, not missing a beat even when her finger was gashed to the bone by a bread slicer.[7] Bandaged up, she soldiered on.

Her devotion to the war effort continued when she visited St. Elizabeth's Hospital, a federal mental-health facility, where she was appalled by the treatment of veterans and the conditions in which they lived. Troubled by the lack of proper care, Eleanor pushed interior secretary Franklin Lane to form a committee to investigate the situation, prompting Congress to increase the hospital's budget.

In 1920, Eleanor accompanied her husband on his unsuccessful campaign for vice president. It was during this whistle-stop campaign that Franklin's campaign advisor, Louis Howe, schooled Eleanor in politics and the press. For Eleanor, this was a transformative time; years later, she said, "I did receive an intensive education on this trip and Louis Howe played a great part in this education from that time on."[8] Still later, when Franklin was elected president in 1932, Howe told Eleanor that in 10 years he could get her elected president.[9] The boast, however, was never tested. Howe died in 1936.

In 1921, the Roosevelts' lives were dramatically altered when Franklin contracted polio on vacation in New Brunswick, Canada. Her husband's travel for various treatments afforded Eleanor time alone, during which she cultivated a political persona and firmly established her reputation as a reformer.[10]

The breach between the Republican Roosevelts of Long Island and the Democrat Roosevelts of the Hudson Valley widened when Franklin and Eleanor opposed cousin Theodore Roosevelt, Jr.'s 1924 gubernatorial bid in New York, choosing instead to support Democrat Al Smith, who won. Campaigning against Ted, Eleanor and her friends pursued him on the campaign trail in a car atop which sat a papier-mâché teapot, intended to suggest a link between Ted and the much-

publicized Teapot Dome bribery scandal of Warren Harding's administration, during which federal oil reserves in California and Wyoming were secretly leased to oil tycoons.[11] Warren himself was never implicated, though his secretary of interior, Albert Fall, was imprisoned for taking a $100,000 bribe.

Months before her husband won the New York State governorship in 1928, Eleanor made clear in a *Red Book Magazine* column – one of many she would write over the course of her life – that when it came to politics, "women must learn to play the game as men do."[12]

"Certain women profess to be horrified at the thought of women bosses bartering and dickering in the hard game of politics with men," she wrote. "But many more women realize that we are living in a material world, and that politics cannot be played from the clouds."[13]

Eleanor's growing interest in politics did not ease her anxieties over becoming first lady. Her memoir would later reveal that on the night of Franklin's presidential election in 1932, she was "more deeply troubled" than she may have let on.[14] "As I saw it, this meant the end of any personal life of my own," she wrote. "I knew what traditionally should lie before me; I had watched Mrs. Theodore Roosevelt and had seen what it meant

to be the wife of the president, and I cannot say that I was pleased at the prospect."[15]

In a moment of candour, Eleanor confided to *Associated Press* reporter and close friend Lorena Hickok, "If I wanted to be selfish, I could wish Franklin had not been elected."[16] However, two days after his inauguration, Eleanor held her first press conference, hosting 35 female journalists to whom she made clear that she valued their position in society, and would provide them access to the White House so that they could "tell the women throughout the country what you think they should know."[17] Throughout her 12 years as first lady, Eleanor held 348 briefings, most of which did not allow men entry.[18]

At a time when the press was a male bastion, Eleanor's evident determination to empower female reporters was a revolutionary act.

Not only did Eleanor engage with the media, she was part of it – writing books, delivering radio broadcasts, and penning a nationally syndicated newspaper column called "My Day" from 1935 to 1962. What started as a six-day-per-

> "The battle for the individual rights of women is one of long standing and none of us should countenance anything which undermines it."

> — ELEANOR ROOSEVELT, 1941

week description of her activities as first lady gradually transformed into a platform from which she could speak on politics – so much so that certain papers dropped the column in 1957, feeling it had become too partisan.[19]

Eleanor brought with her into the White House her determination to tackle the social ills of her era, using her newfound power to call attention to nightmarish conditions in the dilapidated mining town of Scott's Run, West Virginia. Franklin then provided funding for the construction of Arthurdale, an experimental homestead community, though his New Deal package aimed at restoring American prosperity during the Great Depression. Arthurdale was not a complete success, but most of its housing remains in use today.

Early on, the press recognized her advocacy, as evidenced by a 1933 *New Yorker* cartoon that depicted two men shovelling coal deep within a mine, when one remarks, "For gosh sakes, here comes Mrs. Roosevelt!"

Taking her activism further, the first lady allied herself with civil rights, joining the NAACP and lobbying for the Costigan-Wagner Bill that sought to make lynching a federal crime. As well, in a famous act of protest, Eleanor resigned from the Daughters of the American Revolution, a heritage association to which all first ladies were given lifetime memberships, after it refused to allow esteemed black opera singer Marian Anderson to perform in its Constitution Hall in 1939.

During Franklin's 1940 successful re-election bid

for an unprecedented third term, the first lady had become such a recognized figure that she was targeted on campaign pins that read, "And we don't want Eleanor either."[20]

In 1941, Eleanor's influence rose to new heights when she addressed the nation in a radio broadcast following the bombing of Pearl Harbor. Her message of courage and resilience aired before her husband had even spoken publicly on the matter, placing her in a role of leadership previously reserved for the commander-in-chief.

Her tireless activism did not cease after Franklin's sudden death. In 1946, President Harry Truman appointed her chair of the United Nations' Commission on Human Rights, making her instrumental in the drafting of the 1948 Universal Declaration of Human Rights.

She additionally remained a prominent member of the Democratic Party, backing former Illinois governor Adlai Stevenson's 1952 and 1956 failed presidential bids. In 1962, President John F. Kennedy appointed her to chair his Commission on the Status of Women that examined workplace and educational inequality.

Dubbed by President Truman as the "First Lady of the World," Eleanor was an unrelenting advocate for social causes, a voice for the voiceless. She died in 1962 and was interred next to her husband in the Rose Garden at Springwood, the Roosevelts' Hyde Park home. In a memorial address to the UN General Assembly, U.S. ambassador Stevenson lamented that he "lost more than a friend."

"I had lost an inspiration," he said. "For she would rather light candles than curse the darkness and her glow had warmed the world."

OPPOSITE: The president and the first lady pictured on Inauguration Day in 1933.

ELIZABETH VIRGINIA WALLACE TRUMAN

(1885-1982)

FIRST LADY: 12 APRIL 1945-20 JANUARY 1953

Bess Truman, an accidental first lady pushed into the spotlight by her husband's succession following the sudden death of President Franklin Delano Roosevelt, privately played an influential role as her husband's trusted adviser and confidante. Publicly, however, she feared she could never fill her predecessor's shoes.

Born in 1885 in Independence, Missouri, Bess was just five years old when she met Harry Truman at Sunday school in their local Presbyterian church. Harry, who was only one year her senior, later wrote that he "thought she was the most beautiful and the sweetest person on Earth."[1]

After a long courtship, the two married in 1919. Their correspondence revealed their closeness, as Harry told Bess before the wedding, "I haven't any place to go but home and I'm busted financially but I love you as madly as a man can and I'll find all the other things."[2]

The couple's bond spilled over from their personal life into their work life, starting with a men's clothing store, a joint venture that ultimately went bust, and years later with Bess serving as her husband's office clerk on the U.S. Senate payroll – earning her the title "Payroll Bess."[3]

Harry, who spent a decade representing Missouri in the chamber, defended Bess's position while revealing that she was, in effect, his counsellor. "Certainly my wife works for me," he said.[4] "And she earns every cent I pay her. She is my chief advisor. I never write a speech without going over it with her. I have to do that because I have so much

to do and I never make any decisions unless she is in on them. She takes care of my personal mail."[5]

However, when President Roosevelt died abruptly in 1945, just months after Harry became his vice president, Bess expressed no real interest in the first ladyship. The night of Franklin's death, Bess recalled her trepidation about her inevitable future, and the position that would be foisted upon her. "I was very apprehensive," she said. "The country was used to Eleanor Roosevelt. I couldn't possibly be anything like her. I wasn't going down into any coal mines."[6]

Eleanor had left behind a legacy as a celebrated activist, author, and so-called First Lady of the World, and there is no doubt that emulating her tenure would be a herculean feat to this day.

Upon returning from Franklin's funeral, Bess conceded to then-Secretary of Labor Frances Perkins, the first woman to be appointed to the cabinet, "I don't know what I am going to do. I'm not used to this awful public life."[7]

Easing Bess's concerns, Perkins told the first lady that she did not need to hold routine press conferences in the tradition of Eleanor Roosevelt, who had cultivated a relationship with the media and afforded female reporters unprecedented access to the White House. It was a relief.[8] Heeding Perkins' advice, she decided against the briefings, and cancelled the only one she had scheduled.[9] The move was a symbol of the reticence that came to define her tenure and handicapped the media's relationship with the White House, which had

flourished under the Roosevelt administration. When asked by women in the press – whose careers Eleanor had elevated in the male-dominated industry – how they would get to know Bess, she replied, "You don't need to know me. I'm only the president's wife and the mother of his daughter."[10]

Margaret Truman, in her 1986 biography of her mother, cited the first lady's failure "to accept the idea that she too was a public figure as much as the president" as consequential in "one of the nastiest political crossfires" of her husband's presidency.[11]

Scandal erupted when Bess accepted an invitation to tea at Constitution Hall, hosted by heritage organization Daughters of the American Revolution. In 1939, the all-white DAR barred famed black opera singer Marian Anderson from performing at the venue on account of her race. The discrimination prompted Eleanor to publicly resign her membership from the group in protest. The day before the tea, black Congressman Adam Clayton Powell, Jr. urged Bess to reverse her decision, as his wife, pianist Hazel Scott, had also been prohibited from playing a concert at the hall. Neither a segregationist nor a crusader, Bess wouldn't budge, and was backed by her ever-supportive husband, who had endorsed civil rights and had signed an executive order in 1948 to integrate the armed forces.[12]

In retaliation, Powell publicized the response with a searing rebuke of Bess's conduct. "From now on, there is only one First lady, Mrs. Roosevelt," he said. "Mrs. Truman is the last."[13]

Furious, Harry banned Powell from the White House, though he knew his decision to side with his wife "was a mistake," Margaret said.[14] The debacle was an embarrassment to the Truman White House, but evidence of the extent to which Harry, as husband, was protective of his wife. He made that clear during his successful bid for a second term when, on the campaign trail, he introduced Bess as "the Boss."[15]

RIGHT: The president and the first lady attend a football game in 1949.

Bess was, first and foremost, the loving and devoted wife of a husband, a plain-spoken man from Missouri, who became President of the United States; secondarily, she was the first lady of the White House.

"The country was used to Eleanor Roosevelt. I couldn't possibly be anything like her. I wasn't going down into any coal mines."

– BESS TRUMAN

MAMIE GENEVA DOUD EISENHOWER

(1896–1976)

FIRST LADY: 20 JANUARY 1953–20 JANUARY 1961

Born in 1896 in Boone, Iowa, Mamie met Dwight "Ike" Eisenhower just shy of her 19th birthday after her family moved to San Antonio, Texas. The future president was then a West Point graduate and army lieutenant stationed nearby at Fort Sam Houston. In 1916, they married.

Mamie, whose life was moulded around her husband's, took on the traditional role of a military wife. She moved more than two dozen times as he rose through the ranks, serving generals George Moseley, Douglas MacArthur, and George Marshall, who would go on to become President Harry Truman's secretary of state and author of the European economic recovery plan after World War II.

During the war, Ike was appointed commanding general of all American troops in the European theatre, thereby placing Mamie in the public eye. But for Mamie, it was about her husband.

"She's a career woman," *Washington Post* society columnist Elizabeth Henney wrote in 1942. "Her career is 'Ike.'"[1]

Despite their periods of separation, Mamie was stoic, devoting her time as a Red Cross volunteer and a waitress at the Soldiers, Sailors, and Marines Club while scrapbooking new clippings and photos of Ike, whose leadership had earned him notoriety.[2] Henney noted that certain articles were missing quotes from Mamie as she had made a habit of avoiding interviews when possible, "feeling that the glory should be all his."[3]

Mamie, who had overseen the couple's household as her full-time job, became known as a warm and welcoming hostess, a skill for which she was remembered as first lady. "If there has been any one particular characteristic that is outstanding among her homemaking talents, it is her genius for hospitality," Henney wrote.[4] Since their marriage, their residence was fondly called "Club Eisenhower" among friends, the name no doubt a testament to Mamie's ability to create an inviting environment wherever she went.

She brought that same custom to the executive mansion, though when she learned in 1952 that her husband "chose a way of life that would mean permanent fame and entail constant press attention… Mamie was not enthusiastic," her granddaughter-in-law Julie Nixon Eisenhower later recalled.[5]

Mamie exhibited an element of scepticism of the media, as was common among first ladies during their tenure. She was shielded by presidential press secretary Jim Hagerty, who had guarded Ike's image and, by extension, Mamie's.[6] Jim developed a series of rules on handling press enquiries, which Mamie directed him to outline in a 1954 memo to her son as he prepared to be interviewed by a reporter writing a profile of Ike's grandchildren.[7]

"As a precaution, I always talk to any writer first, just to make sure that he or she is all right – that they are not trying to slant their articles or that they have not been planted by someone we wouldn't like to have around," Jim wrote. "We try to keep away from direct quotes and insist that neither the President nor Mrs. Eisenhower are quoted directly."[8]

While she kept her distance from reporters, Mamie

corresponded extensively with the public, becoming America's pen pal. Throughout Ike's two terms in office, she received thousands of letters, sometimes including requests for government assistance, which she forwarded on to the appropriate agencies.[9]

According to presidential historian Gil Troy, Americans "turned to the first lady as a first mother, a crucial ally in making the federal government more nurturing and more human."[10]

Mamie's thoughtful responses to the public were praised by her contemporaries, including future first lady Pat Nixon, who told her, "People are marveling that you have personally signed so much mail, and they are filled with admiration and appreciation."[11]

Stuart Symington, a senator from Missouri, also offered accolades to Mamie's sincerity, stating, "you always write as if you meant it – I suppose that's one of the reasons you have the country in the palm of your hand."[12]

Mamie, whose first ladyship followed a series of politically influential women, broke with the role's changing expectations by returning to its roots of hostess-in-chief while knowing she still had influence over her husband.

In Ike's eight years in the White House, Mamie boasted that she entered the Oval Office just four times, "and each time I was invited."[13]

OPPOSITE: The first lady pictured adjusting a floral arrangement in 1958.

BELOW: The first lady sits in the White House movie theatre with her grandchildren, Barbara Anne, Mary Jean, Susie and David.

TRADITIONAL DUTIES

In the White House, Mamie's first ladyship was defined by her return to the position's traditional duties, which revolved around hostessing, entertaining, and perfecting social graces. As she had during the president's military career, she shied away from media attention, and had no desire to engage heavily with the press. Shortly following the start of her tenure, *The New York Herald Tribune* offered Mamie her own column where she could chronicle her daily life, an idea that mimicked Eleanor Roosevelt's syndicated "My Day" newspaper column.[14] Mamie, unenthused by the prospect, predicted it would be "a terrible chore" and turned it down, disparaging Eleanor's writings in her response.[15] For Mamie, becoming a news item held no appeal, and she had famously described her role in the White House as a mere occupant, stating, "Ike runs the country, and I turn the lamb chops."[16] In fact, Ike trusted her to act as a sounding board on politics and people, seeking her advice as his partner and companion, though she seldom disagreed with his opinions.[17]

JACQUELINE LEE BOUVIER KENNEDY

(1929-94)

Jackie Kennedy's first ladyship has been overwhelmingly defined by its end – the shattering tragedy of her husband's assassination – but her years at his side were a masterclass in image-making, both for her family and the White House.

Jackie was born in 1929 in Southampton, New York, to a Wall Street stockbroker father and a socialite mother, who was an accomplished equestrienne – a skill she passed on to her daughter. After her parents divorced, her mother married Hugh D. Auchincloss Jr., a wealthy stockbroker and lawyer, and relocated with her children to the Washington, D.C. area.

After attending Vassar College and studying in France at the University of Grenoble and the Sorbonne, Jackie graduated from George Washington University with a BA in French literature.

In 1951, she began working as a so-called "inquiring camera girl" for the *Washington Times-Herald*, conducting on-the-street interviews about issues of the day and snapping photos of her subjects.

Around that time, she met then-congressman John F. Kennedy, scion of a wealthy Boston political family, who in 1952 became the junior senator from Massachusetts. In 1953, the couple married and settled in the fashionable Georgetown section of Washington.

When John, often nicknamed Jack, launched his presidential bid in 1960, Jackie was absent from the campaign trail due to her pregnancy and orders from her obstetrician to remain home. However, she rallied enthusiasm for her husband from afar through her "Campaign Wife" syndicated newspaper column distributed by the Democratic National Committee.

The column urged voters to support her husband and asserted that "Jack has always believed that women are vital to a campaign."[1] Her writings were "long on chitchat and short on issues," Maurine Beasley, Philip Merrill College of Journalism professor emerita, states, though she used the space to personally address scepticism of her famously high-fashion wardrobe.[2]

"All the talk over what I wear and how I fix my hair has puzzled me," she remarked. "What does my hairdo have to do with my husband's ability to be President?"[3]

When she became first lady, at age 31, Jackie expressed little interest in politics and, despite her experience in media, kept the press and the public at arm's length. Adamant about keeping media attention away from her two young children, Caroline and John-John, Jackie battled with presidential press secretary Pierre Salinger, who scheduled photography sessions without her knowledge while she was out of town.[4] Despite this reluctance, she maintained some involvement in her husband's push for the presidency. During the campaign, drawing on her fluency in multiple languages, she recorded a television commercial in Spanish targeting Latino voters, especially in Texas.

When it came to her position as first lady, Jackie initially rejected the title, telling the *Saturday Evening Post* that she could not "stand being out in front."[5] "I know it sounds trite, but what I really want is to be behind [John] and to be a good wife and mother."[6]

> "There will be great presidents again,
> but there will never be another Camelot."

– JACKIE KENNEDY, 1963

Instead, she focused her time on a massive White House renovation to pay homage to the country's history. Having already burned through the annual $50,000 decorating budget weeks after Inauguration Day, Jackie established a fine arts committee, hired a curator, and sought to reform legal regulations on tax-deductible donations while seeking out wealthy patrons to foot the bill for her initiative.[7] Eventually, she amassed a more than $1 million trove of antiques and made the executive mansion feel more like home, with a nursery, a private dining room, and an adjoining kitchen.[8] Her refurbishment of the Green Room was more costly than the gross price tag of the Trumans' entire renovation in 1952.[9]

But her work didn't stop there. Jackie also set out to preserve buildings in Washington's historic Lafayette Square. A *Washington Post* article later heralded her efforts as having "rescued the city's history," declaring that she "had a greater effect on the shape and spirit

of the historic heart of the nation's capital than any architect or developer."[10]

Not everyone agreed. Famed architect Ralph Walker, former president of the American Institute of Architects, discounted Jackie's work as an endeavour to "keep on using bad architecture and trying to preserve it," hoping that she "wakes up to the fact that she lives in the twentieth century."[11]

Nonetheless, the first lady's renovations captivated the public. In 1962, the U.S. was given an inside look at the redesigned White House in a tour led by Jackie herself and broadcast on CBS and NBC for an audience of more than four million viewers.[12] Near the end of the programme, John appeared on screen, praising "the great effort that she's made to

ABOVE: Lyndon B. Johnson, accompanied by Jackie, is sworn in as president aboard Air Force One following John F. Kennedy's assassination in 1963.

bring us much more intimately in contact with all the men who lived here."[13]

Jackie also made the arts and culture a hallmark of the Kennedy White House, bringing to Washington noted performers and artists. Collaborating with then French minister of culture André Malraux, she was successful in bringing da Vinci's *Mona Lisa* to the National Gallery of Art for exhibition, on loan from the Louvre.

Widely travelled, Jackie visited a number of foreign countries in the company of her husband on official state visits and on her own, cultivating relationships with various heads of state including Britain's Harold Macmillan, France's Charles de Gaulle, and India's Jawaharlal Nehru.

In 1963, tragedy struck. That August, Jackie gave birth to Patrick Bouvier Kennedy, who died after succumbing to a lung ailment two days later. Then in November, her husband was assassinated while he rode next to her in a motorcade through Dallas, Texas. He was the fourth U.S. president to be murdered in office. As the nation plunged first into shock then into mourning, John's death and Jackie's response to it cemented her vivid image as first lady and gave her eternal life in the American consciousness.

As Vice President Lyndon B. Johnson was sworn in as president aboard Air Force One on the tarmac at Dallas Love Field, Jackie stood stoically at his side in the blood-spattered pink suit she had worn while seated next to her husband. She had refused to take it off, stating, "I want them to see what they have done to Jack."[14]

During her husband's funeral, she again broke with tradition, assuming a more public role in the arrangements and the ceremony than those before her who had faced such a crisis.

A week after John's death, Jackie invited journalist Theodore White to the family's Hyannis Port home, where she was interviewed for an upcoming issue of *Life* magazine that would pay homage to the late president. In speaking of her husband's legacy, Jackie remarked on the acclaimed Broadway musical *Camelot*, which ran from 1960 to 1963, noting that she and the president often listened to its soundtrack.

She said her husband had been especially fond of the verse from the title song: "Don't ever let it be forgot, that once there was a spot, for one brief shining moment that was Camelot."[15] Jackie then said to White, "There will be great presidents again, but there will never be another Camelot."[16]

MUSE AND ICON

The images of Jackie Kennedy reproduced across the media around the time of her husband's assassination and funeral inspired the most famous artist of the century. Andy Warhol had just begun to experiment with images of celebrities – obsessed with the dissemination of information through mass media, he sought to create a visual metaphor for the initial excitement and subsequent devastation of the Kennedy years. Warhol was brought up in the Catholic Church, and the veneration of Jackie as saintly "First Widow" is reflected in his nods to religious art in the gold and blue tones used in many of the 300 Jackie paintings he created.[17]

While Jackie was dismissive of the importance of her style choices, "the Jackie Look" bewitched the world and marked a new era in dressing for public appearances. Having lived in Europe, it's no wonder that her style was more cosmopolitan than all-American – but as first lady, she understood the importance of wearing American designers. Jackie got around this by employing Oleg Cassini, who was unabashedly "inspired" by the European houses of Givenchy, Chanel, and Balenciaga – Jackie's favoured designers. From royalty to Hollywood, nods to her effortless elegance still abound today.

CLAUDIA TAYLOR "LADY BIRD" JOHNSON

(1912–2007)

Lady Bird Johnson dreaded becoming first lady. "I feel as if I am suddenly on stage for a part I never rehearsed," she confessed to a friend in 1963 after moving to the White House in the wake of President John F. Kennedy's assassination.[1]

The nation *had* rehearsed – three times. And despite Lady Bird's claim to the contrary, she did, too, long before entering the executive mansion, and would transform into an activist praised by the press as a "consummate politician."[2]

Claudia Alta Taylor – who earned her iconic name as an infant when a nurse called her "as purty as a ladybird" – met Lyndon B. Johnson in Austin, Texas, in 1934 while he worked for the state's U.S. congressman Richard Kleberg. Lyndon, domineering and decisive, asked for her hand in marriage on the first date. She thought he was joking. Weeks later, they married, arguing on their way into an Episcopal church in San Antonio.[3] As the newlyweds walked out, a doubtful minister reportedly said, "I hope that marriage lasts."[4]

It didn't just last – "they became a Washington institution," journalist and author Kati Marton writes, "she beloved, he feared."[5]

Just as Lyndon was a partner to Lady Bird, she was his helpmate. That was especially true in 1941 when he volunteered to serve in the Navy during World War II and she worked to keep his congressional office open.

After Lyndon entered the Senate in 1949, serving as majority whip, minority leader, and majority leader during his 12-year tenure, Lady Bird

remained his staunch advocate. Taking note of their relationship, Jackie Kennedy, whose husband John F. Kennedy was also a senator at the time, remarked that "Lady Bird would crawl down Pennsylvania Avenue over splintered glass for Lyndon."[6]

As first lady, Lady Bird backed her husband's push for racial equality as he championed the landmark Civil Rights Act of 1964 and later, the Voting Rights Act of 1965. During his presidential bid, when he earned election in his own right, Lady Bird became the first presidential wife to embark on her own whistle-stop campaign. Travelling through eight southern states, she covered more than 1,500 miles in four days.[7] When protesters showed up to speak out against Lyndon's civil rights push, Lady Bird raised her hand and silenced them, stating, "My friends, this is a country of free speech, and I have a respect for your viewpoint. But this is my time to give mine."[8]

Following Lyndon's election win, Lady Bird launched a wide-reaching "beautification" campaign for which her first ladyship became known, though the term doesn't do it justice. The agenda wasn't just cosmetic – it sought to regulate highway billboards, spur urban renewal, push for the expansion of mass transit in Washington, D.C., preserve historic buildings, and improve the overall quality of life. In the words of the president, "beautification" meant "our total concern for the physical and human quality we pass on to our children and the future."[9]

While she had the public support of her husband, the media didn't always frame Lady Bird's work

22 DECEMBER 1912 // Born in Karnack, Texas

1930 // Graduates from St Mary's Episcopal College for Women, Dallas, Texas

1933 // Graduates from the University of Texas with a BA in history, gaining a second BA in 1934

1934 // Meets Lyndon B. Johnson and they marry the same year

1943 // Buys Austin radio station KTBC

1944 // The Johnsons' first daughter, Lynda Bird, is born, followed by Lucy Baines in 1947

1952 // Adds a television station to her business empire – becomes the first first lady to become a millionaire before her husband became president

1963 // Kennedy is assassinated, and Vice President Johnson is inaugurated as president

1964 // Travels across the south in her own train to promote the Civil Rights Act

1970 // Publishes *A White House Diary*, revealing behind-the-scenes details of Johnson's tenure, a year after he leaves office

"I feel as if I am suddenly on stage for a part I never rehearsed."

- LADY BIRD JOHNSON, 1963

with the seriousness it deserved, shortening "beautification" in headlines that read, "First Lady Discusses Beauty" and "A Plea for U.S. Beauty."[10] It didn't help that the articles appeared in society pages aimed at female audiences, now branded by the modern press as lifestyle content.[11]

The first lady's move to spearhead the program further solidified her place in politics as she lobbied for the Highway Beautification Act, dubbed "Lady Bird's Bill." The measure called for a regulatory crackdown on outdoor advertising including the tearing down of certain signs dotting the country's still-developing Interstate Highway System.

When the act stalled in Congress amid resistance from the ad industry, Lyndon, an ally of the plan, told his cabinet: "You know that I love that woman. And she wants that highway beautification bill, and by God, we're going to get it for her!"[12]

In 1965, it passed and was signed into law.

That year, Lady Bird expanded her activism to Lyndon's War on Poverty, inviting to the White House Urie Bronfenbrenner, a Cornell developmental psychologist who helped to develop a federally funded preschool program for impoverished children that became known as Head Start.

Lady Bird, who entered the White House feeling unsure and unrehearsed, left an activist, joining her predecessors who pushed past the role's basic expectations to cultivate the kind of political influence that created a lasting legacy.

As Lyndon once famously declared, voters "would happily have elected her over me."[13]

OPPOSITE: The first lady in 1964 on a whistle-stop campaign for civil rights in the South.

PATRICIA RYAN NIXON

(1912–93)

FIRST LADY: 20 JANUARY 1969–9 AUGUST 1974

Upon becoming first lady, a reporter asked Pat Nixon whether she wanted daughter Tricia to become a politician's wife. "I'd feel sorry for her if she ever married anyone in politics," Pat shot back.[1] She continued that as Richard Nixon's spouse, "had a good life," Pat simply said, "I just don't tell all."[2]

That exchange encapsulated Pat's reaction to her entry into the White House – it happened because of her husband's election and whether she liked it or not, she was in for the ride. But unlike other reluctant first ladies, she participated.

Pat met Richard in 1938 after she graduated from the University of Southern California and became a high school teacher. Initially, "there was no talk of political life at all," she recalled.[3] But once he made up his mind to launch a congressional bid in 1946, Pat felt she had no choice. "The only thing that I could do was to help him, but it would not have been a life that I would have chosen," she said.[4]

At the time, Nixon had just returned from naval service in World War II, and was in Washington, D.C. Pat, despite being several months pregnant with her first child, packed up and headed back to the West Coast to help him launch his campaign. According to historian Mary Brennan, within hours of giving birth, Pat had already gotten back to work typing and researching for Richard's speeches.[5]

His wins were her wins, as were their defeats. In 1960, Richard, having climbed from congressman to senator to vice president under Dwight D. Eisenhower, mounted a challenge to John F. Kennedy's presidential campaign. When he lost, Pat was crestfallen, fighting back tears as he conceded.

The couple eventually made it to the White House in 1969. As first lady, Pat adopted an inherently apolitical platform – volunteerism – declaring, "People are my project."[6] The initiative took her to disadvantaged urban areas and college campuses, where she encouraged charity work.

She used that same humanitarian spirit to become an advocate for the disabled, installing ramps at the White House for accessibility, arranging audio tours for the blind, and training guides to greet hearing-impaired visitors with sign language.

In 1973, as the Watergate scandal began unfolding following her husband's re-election, a Gallup poll ranked her the second-most well-liked woman in the world. While Pat's reputation remained intact, Richard's was crumbling as he faced impeachment due to the 1972 Democratic National Committee headquarters break-in and its subsequent cover-up.

Richard praised her as having been "at her very best when the going was toughest,"[7] but for Pat, it was "the only crisis that ever got me down." Despite the damning evidence against her husband, she maintained that "he was always thinking about the country and not himself."[8]

In 1974, Richard resigned, allowing Pat to breathe what friends described as "an inaudible but very real sigh of relief."[9] Pat made no waves as first lady. Instead, her legacy is as the president's rock, perhaps the only constant as his administration fell apart.

ELIZABETH BLOOMER FORD

(1918 – 2011)

From the moment Betty Ford entered the White House, she refused to be anything but authentic. Gone were the days of image-making and notions of Camelot. There was no pretence. Betty's only promise was to "do the best I can, and if they don't like it, they can kick me out, but they can't make me somebody I'm not."[1]

She didn't expect to become a political wife. After divorcing her first husband, a furniture dealer named William Warren, Betty was engaged in 1948 to Gerald Ford, a lawyer in Grand Rapids, Michigan, who initially hid his hopes of being elected to Congress. Within months of their wedding, he revealed his ambitions. Betty, who admittedly knew nothing about politics, began stuffing envelopes, making phone calls, and recruiting friends to pitch in on his underdog campaign.[2] Three weeks after the couple exchanged their vows, Jerry won in a landslide victory and went on to serve for nearly 25 years.

In 1973, President Richard Nixon tapped Gerald to replace Vice President Spiro T. Agnew, who resigned, mired in tax evasion and bribery scandals. When Nixon stepped down the next year, avoiding likely impeachment in the fallout of Watergate, the Fords moved into the White House. What followed were a series of real and sometimes raw moments that, for part of her tenure, made Betty the most admired woman in the world.[3]

Seven weeks after she became first lady, Betty was diagnosed with breast cancer. Two days later, she underwent a radical mastectomy, then radiation and chemotherapy. Rather than keep her diagnosis a secret, it became the subject of extensive media attention that spurred lifesaving awareness.[4] Thousands of women flooded cancer-screening centres within weeks, having initially been reluctant to receive examinations.[5] One of those women was second lady "Happy" Rockefeller, wife of Vice President Nelson Rockefeller, whose exam led to a double mastectomy. Such operations, once considered taboo topics for discussion, began entering the public conversation, all because Betty didn't shy away.

The famously outspoken first lady lobbied for the ultimately failed Equal Rights Amendment, which aimed to establish equality of the sexes under the Constitution and ban gender discrimination. The measure saw opposition from Republicans, but Betty wasn't about to keep quiet. At the 1975 International Women's Year Conference in Cleveland, she delivered a poignant message: "Why should my husband's job or yours prevent us from being ourselves? Being ladylike does not require silence."[6]

The full extent of Betty's influence in Gerald's administration remains unclear, though she credited herself for the appointments of Housing and Urban Development Secretary Carla Hills and U.S. ambassador to Britain Anne Armstrong, both of whom were the first women to fill their respective roles.

Perhaps the first lady's greatest legacy came

"Why should my husband's job or yours prevent us from being ourselves? Being ladylike does not require silence."

– BETTY FORD, 1975

in 1978 after she left the White House and announced that she had been battling an alcohol and drug addiction. Betty broke the news in a public statement, and checked into Long Beach Naval Hospital in California for treatment.

Instead of keeping quiet on her experience, she chronicled her rehabilitation in *A Glad Awakening*, one of her three memoirs, offering a candid account of her struggle.

In 1982, she established the Betty Ford Center, a recovery facility at Eisenhower Medical Center southeast of Palm Springs, which attracted celebrity alumni including Mickey Mantle, Johnny Cash, and Mary Tyler Moore.

In just three years as first lady, Betty turned the position's long-standing tradition of image-making on its head, by simply being herself and refusing to fit the mould. Doing so not only empowered her to publicly battle cancer and substance abuse, but persuaded numerous other Americans to do the same.

OPPOSITE: The Fords at the 1976 Republican National Convention in Kansas City, Missouri.

RIGHT: The first lady snaps a Polaroid of the presidential photographer at the White House in 1976.

A SOCIALLY LIBERAL AGENDA

Betty wasn't afraid to discuss issues of sex and reproductive rights, voicing her support for landmark supreme court case *Roe v. Wade* during a bombshell *60 Minutes* interview in 1975 with broadcast titan Morley Safer. Making her point, Betty declared it was time to bring abortion "out of the backwoods and put it in the hospitals where it belongs."[7]
She also famously told Safer that she "wouldn't be surprised" if daughter Susan decided to have a premarital affair, noting that she would even offer her advice.[8] Gerald later quipped that in the 1976 election, that line had cost him 20 million votes.[9]
The National Review, a conservative publication, decried the first lady's interview performance, declaring that Betty was "rewriting the Ten Commandments over nationwide TV."[10]
Politically, she had taken a stand as one of the last notable Republicans to embrace social liberalism as the GOP shifted further right under the influence of Ronald Reagan. Soon, her values would become relics of a party that no longer existed.

ROSALYNN SMITH CARTER

(1927 –)

FIRST LADY: 20 JANUARY 1977–20 JANUARY 1981

The daughter of an auto mechanic and a seamstress in the tiny town of Plains, Georgia, Rosalynn Carter rose from small-town girl to president's right-hand woman.

Born in 1927, she grew up just down the street from Jimmy Carter, her best friend's brother. At 17, Rosalynn met Jimmy, a midshipman at the U.S. Naval Academy three years her senior. In 1946, the couple married.

In 1953, against Rosalynn's vehement objections, Jimmy left the Navy and returned home to take over his family's peanut warehouse once his father died. Rosalynn proved a shrewd businesswoman, honing her management skills and helming the operation alongside her husband. Their partnership of equals transformed into a political alliance as Jimmy launched his career, becoming a Georgia state senator in 1963, then governor in 1971, a win propelled in part by Rosalynn's efforts on the campaign trail.

While her husband was in office, Rosalynn championed mental health, joining his Commission to Improve Services to the Mentally and Emotionally Handicapped, through which she pushed for better state resources.

After Jimmy was elected president in 1976, Rosalynn carried that initiative into the White House as the honorary chair of his Commission on Mental Health launched in 1977. The following year, she lobbied for the successful passage of the Mental Health Systems Act, testifying before the Senate on its behalf. The bill, signed into law in 1980, aimed to end unnecessary institutionalization and provided federal grants to community health centres.

Though the legislation was short-lived, being later reversed by the Reagan administration, Rosalynn was confident in her ability to gain the president's support for her agenda. "I think in things like mental health, Jimmy just depends on me to tell him what I think needs to be done," she told *The New York Times* in 1978. "I really do think I have some influence on those things I know about."[1]

Such was the first lady's thinking on an array of issues, from social services to foreign policy. At weekly working lunches, the couple mulled over political appointments, the status of various bills in Congress, and the latest developments in the Middle East, saving chitchat for supper.[2] Rosalynn had even attended cabinet meetings, not as a participant but as an observer gathering insights into the goings-on of her husband's administration.

Rosalynn also played the role of ambassador, serving as an emissary to Latin America and the Caribbean, where she traveled on a 13-day swing in 1977, meeting with heads of state to talk trade and defence. Upon her return, she was met with a mix of applause and scrutiny for her diplomatic work.

Meanwhile, the institution of the first lady was becoming more formally recognized, as Rosalynn was the first to establish her own workspace in the East Wing, now known as the Office of the First Lady. Her position was given further authority with

the 1978 passage of Public Law 95–750, which linked the first lady's position to that of her husband. Under the measure, funds were allocated for upkeep of the executive mansion as well as "assistance and services" provided to first ladies in connection with the president's duties.[3]

Just as Congress acknowledged the first lady's standing, so did Jimmy, who called Rosalynn "a very equal partner" and "a perfect extension of myself."[4] With her influence came criticism from the public and the press, which questioned the first lady's power, labelling her "the Assistant President."[5] In response to a reporter who noted that unlike Jimmy's peanut farm, the White House did not belong to his family, Rosalynn argued, "In a way, the American voter does elect the family."[6] As a 1979 *Newsweek* cover story put it, "the real fear of Rosalynn's power may lie simply in the fact that she is an ambitious woman."[7]

That became especially apparent in 1980 amid the Iranian hostage crisis in which the U.S. Embassy in Tehran was raided and more than 50 Americans were held captive. As the president remained in Washington, D.C. to handle the fiasco, Rosalynn campaigned solo for his re-election, attending fundraisers and primaries in his place. However, trouble abroad coupled with a faltering economy and divisions within the Democratic Party signalled his ultimate defeat by Ronald Reagan.

Rosalynn, who broke down in tears over the loss, told *The Washington Post* days later, "I worked very hard to stay here, but I didn't get to," adding, "I don't feel bitter towards the American people. I don't see it at all as a rejection of Jimmy Carter. I see it as a protest vote, and I can understand their feelings."[8]

LEFT: Betty Friedan, Liz Carpenter, First Lady Rosalynn Carter, former first lady Betty Ford, Elly Peterson, Jill Ruckelshaus, and Bella Abzug attend the 1977 National Women's Conference in Houston, Texas to promote the Equal Rights Amendment.

NANCY DAVIS REAGAN

(1921–2016)

Glamorous, outspoken, and influential, Nancy Reagan emerged as the power behind the throne during her husband's administration, her apparently outsize role outshining many of her predecessors.

Born in 1921 in the New York City borough of Queens, to an actress, and a car dealer father who deserted the family when Nancy was a child, she decided to follow in her mother's footsteps and pursue a film career. In 1949, she moved to Hollywood, California, on a seven-year contract with Metro-Goldwyn-Mayer studios, and scored several roles including the lead in *The Next Voice You Hear.* That same year, as the so-called Red Scare targeted the entertainment industry, Nancy found her name had mistakenly landed on a list of accused Communist sympathizers and called Ronald Reagan, who was then head of the Screen Actors Guild, for help. The two met for dinner and, after an on-and-off courtship, married in 1952.

The Reagans' relationship was widely viewed as a fairytale romance, the couple having appeared to be deeply in love long after their wedding day. It was also a political alliance that was seen as key to Ronald's eventual rise to the White House.

In the 1960s, Ronald entered into politics, switching his party affiliation from Democrat to Republican. The change was frequently attributed to the conservative influence of Nancy and her stepfather, though she denied that was the case, arguing that her husband chose his own path.[1]

In 1966, Ronald was elected governor of California, a seat he held for two terms. In 1980, he was elected president. Ronald's former aide and longtime friend, Michael Deaver, said neither win would have happened without Nancy.[2] During his failed 1976 presidential bid, she helped to hire and fire her husband's political consultants, just as she did in 1980. That included campaign manager John Sears, who was ousted that year amid Nancy's concerns that he cared more for his own image than that of her husband.[3]

As first lady, she exercised the same degree of influence, engineering the firing of Chief of Staff Donald Regan, who had previously served as the president's treasury secretary. At the heart of the matter was the 1986 Iran-Contra affair in which the U.S., despite an embargo, secretly sold arms to Iran in exchange for the release of seven hostages in Lebanon, and used the proceeds to provide weapons to insurgents known as the Contras, who were opposing Nicaragua's leftist government. In 1987, a report from the Tower Commission led by former senator John Tower, a Republican, slammed Ronald for an apparent lack of understanding of the disastrous deal, and placed blame also on his aides, including Donald. Donald urged the president, who was recovering from prostate cancer surgery, to get back into the public eye and address the scandal in a news conference. The first lady opposed the idea, advising her husband to lay low and deliver a scripted apology – a more controlled message. She even sought backup from former Democratic National Committee chair Robert Strauss, whom she asked to convince Ronald that his reputation

would be jeopardized if he remained silent.[4]

Nancy's power over the president prompted *New York Times* columnist William Safire to compare her to Edith Wilson, Woodrow Wilson's second wife who all but ran the Oval Office when he had a severe stroke in 1919, and according to most should have resigned. After Donald's firing, the writer berated Nancy as "presuming to control the actions and appointments of the executive branch."[5] However, other witnesses to history saw it differently. Margaret Warner, a journalist

ABOVE: Nancy Reagan pictured dancing with her husband, date unknown.

OPPOSITE: Nancy at a Just Say No rally, 1988.

who had covered Ronald's presidential campaign for the *San Diego Union*, praised Nancy as "tough, insightful and shrewd about what her husband needed in support to actually shine."[6]

Ronald eventually decided to give a televised *mea culpa* for the Iran-Contra deal as Nancy suggested, and subsequently saw reinvigorated approval ratings.

The first lady had long been the president's protector, dating back to when he was shot in a 1981 assassination attempt on his life. From that moment on, according to Nancy's 1989 memoir, *My Turn*, she lived in constant fear for his safety, so much so that she enlisted astrologer Joan Quigley to oversee parts of his schedule.[7] Joan later claimed to have chosen the timing of press conferences, State of the Union speeches, and flights on Air Force One, though Nancy claimed political decisions were never based on the stars.[8]

JUST SAY NO

Nancy's first ladyship was somewhat defined by her anti-drug and alcohol-addiction platform, taglined "Just Say No." The initiative, launched during the first of Ronald's two terms, saw her travel around the nation and abroad, presenting speeches discouraging substance abuse. Though the program was criticized as overly simplistic and ineffectual, the movement continued for more than a decade, the slogan making its way into ad campaigns.

The first lady had weathered further scrutiny of her style, having attracted attention for her high-fashion ensembles and friendships with big-name designers James Galanos and Oscar de la Renta. Writer Joan Didion delivered an especially scathing portrayal in her 1968 *Saturday Evening Post* profile of Nancy, whom she described as having "the smile of a woman who seems to be playing out some middle-class American woman's daydream, circa 1948...perfectly dressed, every detail correct."[9]

Nancy's "biggest fault," the first lady later wrote of herself, was that she "was too polite, too much a lady."[10] But in the White House, from her partnership with Ronald to her involvement in his selection of staff as well as their dismissals, she proved that she stood toe-to-toe with any man, even the president.

BARBARA PIERCE BUSH

(1925–2018)

FIRST LADY: 20 JANUARY 1989–20 JANUARY 1993

For a White House whose previous East Wing occupant was a film actress, friend to fashion designers, and ardent political ally to her husband, Barbara Bush was heralded as a breath of fresh air.

"Now for Something Completely Different: A Down-to-Earth First Lady," a 1989 *Time* magazine headline read, dubbing white-haired Barbara "the silver fox."[1]

While she refused to fixate on the image-making tactics that marked the eras of Kennedy and Reagan, Barbara's ability to relate to the average American contrasted with her well-heeled upbringing in a life of privilege.

Born in 1925 in New York City, Barbara grew up in the suburban town of Rye, attending Ashley Hall boarding school in South Carolina. While at a Greenwich, Connecticut country club dance during her Christmas break in 1941, she met George H. W. Bush, a senior at Phillips Academy in Andover, Massachusetts. Less than two years later, they were engaged. George then went off to serve in World War II as a Navy torpedo bomber pilot, and upon his return on leave, the couple married in 1945.

The Bushes set out for Texas, where George launched an oil business then entered politics, serving two terms in Congress after which he was appointed U.S. ambassador to the United Nations. He went on to chair the Republican National Committee, headed up the Central Intelligence Agency, then became vice president under the Reagan administration, making Barbara second lady for eight years. The couple had six children, turning them into the leaders of a political dynasty – one served as president and another was elected governor of Florida.

Barbara wasn't just the family matriarch. For a time, she was the nation's – becoming affectionately known as "everybody's grandmother." In an interview roughly two weeks before her husband's presidential inauguration, she told *The Washington Post* that her rise to first lady at age 63 had inspired the public. "My mail tells me a lot of fat, white-haired, wrinkled ladies are tickled pink," she said. "I think it makes them feel better about themselves. I mean, look at me – if I can be a success, so can they."[2]

As presidential historian Gil Troy later wrote, "the less interested she seemed in power, the more she seemed to get."[3]

But Barbara made no overt attempts to exercise power. Instead, she avoided discussing politically fraught topics, and did not publicly break with the president's positions. Asked by a reporter about whether she backed the Equal Rights Amendment championed by certain of her predecessors, she declined to pick a side. "I want equal rights for women, men, everybody, equal rights for every American, equal pay for equal work," she said, adding, "I'm not against it or for it. I'm not talking about it."[4]

It was suspected that she believed in abortion rights despite her husband's opposition, though she did not address the matter during his presidency. It wasn't until after her death in 2018 that *USA Today* Washington bureau chief Susan Page revealed that

OPPOSITE: The president and first lady at the 1989 inauguration celebration.

ABOVE : The first lady visits U.S. Marines stationed in Saudi Arabia during the Gulf War, on Thanksgiving 1990.

she had seen journal writings in which Barbara had privately debated the question, deciding to support federally funded abortions and declaring that the government had no place in controlling the procedure via legislation.[5]

In a rare and widely quoted exception to her apolitical persona, Barbara in 1988 called Geraldine Ferraro, the Democratic vice presidential nominee who had run against George, something that "rhymes with rich."[6] While she later regretted the slight, Terence Hunt, the Associated Press reporter who heard it, contended that it proved "her grandmotherly white hair and fake pearls were deceiving.... She was intimidating, no one to mess with."[7]

In a 1992 interview with the *Los Angeles Times*, Barbara suggested that she did have some sway over the president despite not participating much

in his work, though it was by virtue of their long relationship. "You have to have influence," she said. "When you've been married 47 years, if you don't have any influence, then I really think you're in deep trouble."[8]

Generally, however, Barbara kept out of politics, spearheading efforts to combat illiteracy across the country through her Barbara Bush Foundation for Family Literacy, which she founded in 1989. The organization raised funds for family literacy programs and supported teacher training, drawing links between poverty, poor health, crime, and reading and writing abilities. In 1990, the first lady hosted "Mrs. Bush's Story Time," a 10-part evening radio show in which she read children's books.

Imagining the legacy she would leave behind, Barbara wrote in 1988 that she wished "to be known as a wife, a mother, a grandmother."[9]

"That's what I am," she added. "And I'd like to be known as someone who really cared about people and worked very, very hard to make America more literate."[10]

HILLARY RODHAM CLINTON

(1947–)

FIRST LADY: 20 JANUARY 1993–20 JANUARY 2001

Hillary Clinton, a political lightning rod whose reputation nearly eclipses that of her husband, earned her place among the most controversial first ladies in U.S. history by giving the role more authority than it had seen since the days of Eleanor Roosevelt.

Born in Chicago, Illinois, in 1947, Hillary made her first national news splash when graduating from Wellesley College where she was the first student to ever give a commencement speech. She had prepared remarks, though after hearing Republican senator Edward Brooke of Massachusetts – the chamber's only black member – deliver what she deemed a defence of Richard Nixon's presidency, Hillary scrapped her notes and scolded the lawmaker.[1]

In her rebuke, she said Brooke's message was emblematic of "rhetoric we've been hearing for years," challenging leaders to "practice politics as the art of making possible what appears impossible."[2]

The speech earned her a mention in *Life* magazine, and a dismissive review from the *Chicago Tribune*, which called the 21-year-old woman a "girl."[3] A subsequent editorial chastised her "discourtesy" to the senator, calling it "unjust."[4]

It was an early sign of the criticism Hillary would generate as a politically outspoken figure who, rather than play second fiddle to her husband's career, was determined to forge one of her own and make a mark while doing it.

In 1969, Hillary enrolled at Yale Law School and joined the editorial board of the *Yale Review of Law and Social Action*, a student-run quarterly. She met Bill Clinton the following year, finding a commonality in their political ambitions as both travelled to Texas to work on George McGovern's presidential campaign in the summer of 1972.

In 1974, the year after her graduation, Hillary was hired as a staff attorney for the House Judiciary Committee as Congress weighed Nixon's impeachment. However, he resigned that same year, thus concluding her work. In 1975, Hillary and Bill were married. It wasn't long before Bill began climbing the political ladder, first as attorney general of his Arkansas home state, then as its governor – an election he won five times.

Meanwhile, Hillary chaired the Legal Services Corporation under the Carter administration, and practiced at Little Rock's Rose Law Firm, one of Arkansas' best. In 1980, she gave birth to the Clintons' only child, Chelsea.

In 1992, Bill's presidential bid placed the couple on the campaign trail, where the candidate faced his first scandal – a 12-year affair alleged by singer and state government employee Gennifer Flowers. Seated alongside Bill, who vehemently denied the accusation, Hillary's response to CBS News' *60 Minutes* was a preview of another she'd provide when presented with the same story years later.

"I'm not sitting here, some little woman standing by my man," she famously said. "I'm sitting here because I love him and I respect him, and I honor what he's been through and what we've been through together."[5] To Americans sceptical of her husband, Hillary had a simple message: "Heck, don't vote for him."[6]

26 OCTOBER 1947 // Born in Chicago, Illinois

1969 // Graduates from Wellesley College, with departmental honours in political science

1973 // Graduates from Yale Law School

1975 // Marries Bill Clinton.

1979 // Becomes first woman to be made full partner at Rose Law Firm. Named one of 100 most influential US lawyers in *The National Law Journal* in 1988 and 1991

1992 // Bill nominated for Democratic presidential candidate, taking office in 1993

1993 // Becomes chair of task force on National Health Care Reform

1998 // The Lewinsky scandal precedes the president's impeachment and subsequent departure from the White House

2000 // Voted in as US senator of New York.

2008 // Runs for Democratic presidential candidacy, losing to Barack Obama.

2009–2013 // Serves as secretary of state.

2016 // Runs as Democratic presidential candidate, losing to Donald Trump.

As historian Myra Gutin later wrote, it was a motif seen time and again throughout Bill's presidency – he "would err; Hillary would go on the attack and help formulate a strategy to resurrect her husband; he would survive; and all would be forgiven."[7]

Indeed the pattern played out when Bill won the election and the controversy faded from the country's consciousness as the duo moved into the White House. Within days, the first lady was selected to head up the president's Task Force on National Health Care Reform, which was tasked with an overhaul.

Hillary's appointment as its architect fuelled questions over violations of federal nepotism laws, which had been instituted after President John F. Kennedy tapped his brother for attorney general. Initially, a federal judge ruled that the first lady was neither an "official" nor an "employee," despite the White House's claim that she was the "functional equivalent" of an administrative staffer.[8] As a result, the task force was defined as an advisory commission, meaning it had to open its meetings to the public. Several months later, a federal appeals court ruled that Hillary was a "de facto" government official and approved her panel's secrecy.[9]

For the role of the first lady, the court's decision blurred the boundaries of the title that was once merely ceremonial.

With the help of Bill's senior policy advisor, Ira Magaziner, the first lady championed the Health Security Act, nicknamed "Hillarycare," a plan to deliver universal health insurance by marrying the free market with federal regulations. The 1,342-page bill was widely seen as an immensely complex proposal crafted by eggheads who gave lawmakers a barely comprehensible explanation as to how it would function.[10] It did not pass, but Hillary's role in its introduction built on existing precedents for the involvement of a first lady in developing legislation.

The Clintons faced a list of additional scandals that tainted Bill's and, by extension, Hillary's reputations, the granddaddy of which became known as Whitewater – a controversy over their financial contributions to a real estate development firm during Bill's time as governor. Investigations found no criminal wrongdoing by the Clintons, though their investment partners were convicted of fraud. The dust-up was followed by the so-called Travelgate debacle in which seven White House travel office employees were fired over alleged ethics failures and mismanagement of financial records. The Clintons were accused of pushing out federal staffers to free up spots for cronies, but those who investigated the matter found no reason to bring charges, and most of the employees were later rehired.

In 1998, Bill faced accusations of a sexual relationship with White House intern Monica Lewinsky – the one scandal he couldn't survive – and Hillary again came to his defense. In an interview on the *Today Show*, she claimed it was "part of a continuing political campaign against my husband," noting that both she and the president had faced numerous allegations before and that the truth would come to light eventually.[11]

It did, but only after Bill had stated under oath that he did not have sex with Monica, and later admitted to it, which resulted in his impeachment. The Senate then acquitted him, allowing the president to serve out his term until 2001.

In 1999, Hillary began pursuing her own political aims, launching a successful run for a Senate seat representing New York, and in effect, redefining what it meant to be first lady. While campaigning, she filled the role part-time, showing that presidential wives had the power to be more than helpmates for their husband's administrations.

While Americans initially reacted with disbelief at the thought of the first lady as senator,[12] Hillary's bid turned out to be only the start of a career rivalling Bill's – including a secretary of state post under the Obama administration, and two presidential runs in 2008 and 2016, albeit they were unsuccessful.

Unlike those before her, Hillary turned her first ladyship into the start of a political journey separate from her husband's, charting new territory with Senate and White House bids, and redefining the place of presidential spouses in U.S. politics.

LAURA WELCH BUSH

(1946 -)

Noncontroversial and famously reluctant, Laura Bush's success as first lady lay in her ability to fly under the radar as her husband's supporter, maintaining high approval ratings even as his sunk under the weight of the war in Iraq and a faltering economy at home.

Born in Midland, Texas, in 1946, Laura met George W. Bush in 1977 through mutual friends at a barbecue, marrying him the same year. As a precondition to their nuptials, George, who was then staking a career in the oil industry, promised Laura she would never have to make a stump speech, should he pursue politics.[1]

Though Laura was hesitant to play any role in her husband's career aims, the agreement became nothing more than a humorous anecdote once he launched his gubernatorial campaign. He won two terms, in 1994 and 1998, during which she frequently delivered public remarks.[2]

For Laura, a former librarian and elementary-school teacher, political life was a dramatic shift from the relatively private life she had once led. But following her husband's presidential election, Laura would slowly emerge as a quietly powerful first lady who, due to her likability, was an asset to George when his administration became the target of scrutiny.

In 2001, roughly two months after the September 11 terror attacks, Laura made history as the first woman in her role to ever take over the president's weekly radio address. She delivered a strong denunciation of the oppression of women and children in Afghanistan under Taliban rule, calling out the brutal regime and its denial of education to female citizens.[3]

Further championing education as her prime initiative, Laura testified before the Senate in 2002 on the importance of literacy, pointing to twin daughters Jenna and Barbara, whom the Bushes taught to read early on.[4]

Her performance stood in stark contrast to that of Hillary Clinton, for example, who had previously testified in defence of her hotly debated healthcare plan. Rather than adopting a politically charged platform, Laura had chosen one that all of America could get behind, carefully speaking from prepared remarks while making her case to lawmakers.[5]

Unlike certain of her predecessors, Laura undertook numerous projects throughout her tenure, raising awareness of the dangers of drug and alcohol abuse among young people, the value of a healthy diet and exercise, and the risks of heart disease and breast cancer. She also pushed for the No Child Left Behind Act (NCLB) that established a system under which the federal government monitored educational gaps and held schools accountable.

With the exception of subsequent criticism of NCLB for its failure to consider the cases of individual students instead of judging schools by uniform standards,[6] the bill passed with bipartisan support, and the remainder of Laura's agenda was practically apolitical in nature.

It was a surprise in 2004 when, during her husband's bid for re-election, a seemingly more polished, more savvy Laura emerged as his "stealth campaigner," as *The New York Times* put it.[7] Travelling alongside secret service agents, the first lady began solo barnstorming in key states, her superpower being that she rose above politics, which made her consistently well liked by the public.[8]

In 2006, Gallup reported that more than 80 per cent of the nation approved of her job;[9] meanwhile his approval rating hovered above 40 per cent.[10] By 2008, in the final days of his term, it had plummeted to less than 30 per cent.[11]

It wasn't until after leaving the White House that Laura's political positions became more apparent with the 2010 release of her memoir, *Spoken from the Heart*, and a series of interviews to promote it. Speaking to famed television host Larry King, Laura showed her support for same-sex marriage and abortion – both of which her husband opposed and took action against while in office.[12]

While she evidently didn't sway his opinion on either, she *did* influence his decision to quit drinking – another matter she addressed with candour after his presidency ended. "I was not going to leave George and I wasn't going to let him leave me with twins," she wrote in her memoir. "Our marriage was enduring, we loved each other, and we were two people who did not have divorce in our DNA. But I was disappointed and I let him know that I thought he could be a better man."[13]

Laura, while not politically influential within her husband's administration, helped to shape him into the candidate he became, and, during his tenure, served as its bright spot, garnering public admiration and advocating for unifying causes.

ABOVE: Laura Bush in 2007 at the Sheikh Khalifa Medical Centre in Abu Dhabi, where she met with women in the Pink Majlis, a forum focusing on breast cancer awareness.

OPPOSITE: The first lady meets with Hurricane Katrina survivors in 2005 at the Cajundome arena in Lafayette, Louisiana.

"We talk about issues, but I'm not his adviser, I'm his wife ... I find that it's really best not to give your spouse a lot of advice. I don't want a lot of advice from him."

– LAURA BUSH, 2004

MICHELLE LAVAUGHN ROBINSON OBAMA

(1964 –)

FIRST LADY: 20 JANUARY 2009–20 JANUARY 2017

Michelle Obama branded herself as America's "mom-in-chief,"[1] winning public approval with candour about balancing family with life in the White House, caring for her two daughters, and the wellbeing of the nation through fitness-focused initiatives.

Born in 1964 in Chicago, Illinois, Michelle excelled in high school and received her undergraduate degree from Princeton University, where she spearheaded a reading program for the children of the campus's manual labourers. Not until the 2018 release of her memoir, *Becoming*, did she detail the division between the school's "extremely white and very male" body and students of colour such as herself.[2] "If in high school I'd felt as if I were representing my neighborhood, now at Princeton I was representing my race," she wrote. "Anytime I found my voice in class or nailed an exam, I quietly hoped it helped make a larger point."[3]

Michelle went on to graduate from Harvard Law School in 1988, then joined corporate Chicago law firm Sidley Austin, where she specialized in intellectual property and marketing. While there, she was assigned as an adviser to Barack Obama, a summer associate three years her senior who was finishing law school. The two married in 1992.

Leaving law for public service, Michelle entered Chicago's City Hall as assistant commissioner of planning and development to Mayor Richard Daley in 1991. Two years later, she launched the city's chapter of Public Allies, a social justice

organization developed under the AmeriCorps federal volunteer program.

In 1996, Michelle combined her passion for volunteer work with academia, joining the University of Chicago as its associate dean of student services and developing its community service program. That year, Barack made a successful run for Illinois State Senate, giving Michelle her first taste of the campaign trail as she collected signatures and arranged fundraisers to aid her husband's bid.

In 2002, partway through Barack's time as a state senator, Michelle began serving in leadership positions at the school's medical centre, acting as a liaison with Chicago's South Side community. As she pursued a high-paying and ambitious career, Michelle had daughters Malia, born in 1998, and Sasha, born in 2001. Meanwhile, Barack continued climbing the political ladder, winning election to the U.S. Senate in 2005 and subsequently running for president in 2008.

During Barack's campaign, Michelle proved to be an asset in currying favour among voters, with her blunt remarks characterized by a lack of pretence, so much so that she had once been seen as a potential liability.[4] But rather than handicapping Barack, her authenticity, allowing her to relate to a broad swath of Americans with her working-class roots and experiences as a busy mother, gave him an edge.[5] Her ability to convince undecided voters to support Barack earned her the nickname "the closer,"[6] showing that his campaign recognized

17 JANUARY, 1964 // Born in Chicago, Illinois, to Fraser and Marian Shields Robinson.

1981–85 // Attends Princeton University, majoring in sociology and minoring in African American studies. Graduates cum laude.

1988 // Graduates from Harvard Law School.

1989 // In her first job as an attorney at Sidley & Austin, Chicago, she meets her mentee and future husband – Barack Obama.

1991 // Leaves legal profession to work as assistant to Chicago mayor Richard Daley, going on to become assistant commissioner of planning and development.

1998 // The Obamas have their first daughter, Malia. Their second daughter, Sasha is born in 2001.

2009 // Barack wins the presidency, and Michelle becomes first lady. The Obamas are the first African American first family in US history.

2010 // Launches national campaign Let's Move! with the goal of reducing childhood obesity.

2011 // Launches Joining Forces with Dr Jill Biden, a campaign for national veterans.

2015 // Launches Let Girls Learn, an international campaign for girls' access to education.

2016 // Appears on the cover of Vogue magazine for the third time.

2018 // Her memoir Becoming is published and becomes an immediate bestseller, going on to sell over 10 million copies.

"Success isn't about how much money you make, it's about the difference you make in people's lives"

– MICHELLE OBAMA, 2012

ABOVE: Michelle Obama at London's Mulberry School for Girls in 2015 speaking to students while on an international tour for her Let Girls Learn initiative.

and understood her role in securing his win. She wasn't only a talented lobbyist – she knew how to talk politics, giving lengthy speeches on a range of foreign and domestic matters, including the U.S.'s problematic military strategy in Iraq and the flaws of George W. Bush's No Child Left Behind Act.[7]

As first lady, she became an advocate for education through her Reach Higher Initiative and Let Girls Learn program, which pushed for educational achievement at home and abroad. However, her greatest legacy remains her "Let's Move!" campaign against childhood obesity, which promoted healthy eating and exercise. Framing the initiative in personal terms – again embracing her signature candour – Michelle cited her daughters' weight gain as her motive for encouraging not just her family but the country as a whole to take stock of its habits. In the project's first year, Michelle prioritized the passage of the Healthy, Hunger-Free Kids Act to make school lunches more nutritious and expand access to meals at little to no cost for students. The bill, which the president signed into law at the end of 2010, placed Michelle on a still-short list of first ladies who were instrumental in legislative action.

The first lady herself evidently took fitness seriously, showing off her muscular arms in sleeveless outfits that made headlines. "Nancy Reagan wore spangled ballgowns. Barbara Bush had fake pearls. Michelle Obama wears her bare arms," *The New York Times's* Jodi Kantor wrote in 2009, reciting the first lady's extensive workout routine that came complete with cardio, weights, and a personal trainer.[8]

Michelle embraced the statement-making look in numerous public appearances, including at the 2012 Democratic National Convention, where she campaigned for her husband's re-election and spoke openly about her effort to play the role of parent and first lady while keeping her children out of the political fray.

From her outfits to her speeches, Michelle, while maintaining an element of privacy in her family life, did not hide who she was, and knew the power of sincerity in garnering public approval. She used the same approach when it came to social media and television, whether belting out Beyoncé on late-

ABOVE: The Obamas dance at the National Governors Association dinner in 2009 in the White House's State Dining Room.

night comedian James Corden's *Carpool Karaoke* or dancing on *The Ellen DeGeneres Show.*[9]

Over the course of her eight years as first lady, Michelle had so elevated her public image and her approval rating that she spurred calls for a presidential run, though she repeatedly declined.

In 2017, stepping down from her post and addressing the nation's youth as it prepared for the inauguration of President-elect Donald Trump, Michelle said her final message was simple:

"I want our young people to know that they matter, that they belong ... Don't be afraid, be focused. Be determined. Be hopeful. Be empowered. Empower yourself with a good education ... then build a country worthy of your boundless promise."[10]

MELANIA
TRUMP

(1970 -)

Melania Trump, the notoriously private wife of one of the most controversial American presidents, remains a subject of public fascination and speculation among those who wondered who the first lady was behind closed doors.

Melania was born in 1970 in the small town of Novo Mesto, Slovenia, to a travelling car salesman and a farmhand-turned-textile-industry worker. Her father, who belonged to the Communist Party at a time when membership could advance ambitious careers regardless of ideology, has drawn comparisons to Donald Trump for his outsize personality and swagger, complete with a Mercedes and a Maserati.[1]

Like both Melania's father and her eventual husband, her mother was conscious of the family's appearance, sewing clothes for her two daughters and making sure they were smartly dressed.[2]

Following high school, Melania traded architecture school for modelling and Germanized her name from Melanija Knavs to Melania Knauss. Her career eventually landed her in New York City, where she met Donald Trump at Manhattan's Kit Kat Club. Initially rejecting his request for her phone number as he arrived at the venue with another woman, Melania eventually ended up dating Donald; the two became engaged in 2004 and married the year after.

While Melania was neither a staunch nor constant defender of her husband's administration amid its myriad scandals, she has attempted to justify his controversial behaviour. In one such instance, she appeared on a 2011 episode of *The Joy Behar Show* after Donald had added his voice to a racist and debunked birther conspiracy aimed at then-President Barack Obama, which questioned the Hawaii-born leader's U.S. citizenship. Melania asserted that "it would be very easy" for Obama to show his birth certificate, claiming that "American people who voted for him and who didn't voted [sic] for him. . . want to see that!"[3]

The remarks represent one of a limited number of instances in which Melania has waded into politics. In 2016, nearly a year before her husband's election, she told *Harper's Bazaar* that she was "choosing not to go political in public because that is my husband's job."[4]

"I'm very political in private life, and between me and my husband I know everything that is going on," she said. "I follow from A to Z. But I chose not to be on the campaign. I made that choice. I have my own mind. I am my own person, and I think my husband likes that about me."[5]

However, Melania became the face of a major political embarrassment when speaking at the Republican National Convention that year when it was realized that part of her speech was nearly identical to the one First Lady Michelle Obama delivered in 2008 at the Democratic convention. Rushing that time to her own defence, Melania made a rare television appearance on NBC News, claiming to have written it "with as little help as possible."[6]

Unlike other first ladies but much like her

> ## "I am not a 'yes' person. No matter who you are married to, you still need to lead your life. I don't want to change him, and he doesn't want to change me."
>
> – MELANIA TRUMP, 2016

husband, Melania was entering into a world in which she had no experience, making her, as Kati Marton, author of *Hidden Power: Presidential Marriages That Shaped Our History*, stated, "the least prepared first lady in history."[7]

Melania's influence in the White House remained difficult to discern throughout her tenure, as she kept much of her life out of the public eye. In 2018, she disappeared from view for weeks after undergoing kidney surgery, prompting the media to label her "missing."[8] At the start of 2019, she again disappeared, making no appearances as her spokesperson said she was planning for her work in the new year.[9]

That included her "Be Best" initiative launched in 2018 to encourage children's wellbeing by advocating against substance abuse and online bullying. The platform was widely seen as a contradiction to Donald's presidency, as he became infamous for browbeating his critics, journalists, and even world leaders. In 2019, he made headlines by challenging teenage climate activist Greta Thunberg on Twitter, calling it "ridiculous" that she was named *Time* magazine's Person of the Year and accusing her of having an "anger management" problem.[10]

As scepticism grew over Melania's silence, her spokesperson said the first lady and the president "often communicate differently," adding that by comparison, their 13-year-old son, Barron, who

has faced cyberbullying, "is not an activist who travels the globe giving speeches."[11]

The implicit rationalization for Donald's behavior became a hallmark of Melania's public statements – the few that were issued – in which she commented on matters involving the president.

Conversely, Melania took a clear and ardent stance on media coverage of the White House, openly sharing in Donald's frustration with and contempt for reporters. In a 2018 interview with Fox News opinion host Sean Hannity, one of her husband's allies, Melania declared that journalists were "opportunists who are using my name or my family name to advance themselves."[12]

While it is unclear the extent to which Melania's views shape and are shaped by those of her husband, that year she expressed disapproval in a public statement of Mira Ricardel, a deputy national security adviser, just one day before the official was ousted. In 2019, *Free, Melania*, an unauthorized biography of the first lady written by CNN reporter Kate Bennett, stated that it was Melania who had chosen to fire the White House's chief usher, whom her predecessor hired.[13]

On whether she truly had the ability to sway Donald's views, Melania told *Harper's Bazaar* in 2016 that she offers her opinions, "and sometimes he takes them in, and sometimes he does not."[14]

"Do I agree with him all the time? No," she conceded. "I think it is good for a healthy relationship. I am not a 'yes' person. No matter who you are married to, you still need to lead your life. I don't want to change him. And he doesn't want to change me."[15]

OPPOSITE: The president and the first lady touring the aftermath of Hurricane Michael in 2018 in Lynn Haven, Florida.

JILL
BIDEN
(1951-)

Three decades in education, eight years as second lady and now having entered a new role as first lady, Jill Biden may become the only woman to break from tradition, planning to hold that title while holding a salaried position of her own as a professor.

Born in New Jersey in 1951, Jill grew up in suburban Philadelphia as the oldest of five sisters. It wasn't until 1975 that she met Joe Biden while still a college senior at the University of Delaware. At the time, Joe was already serving as a U.S. senator, and had lost his wife, Neilia, and their 1-year-old daughter, Naomi, in a Christmastime car crash in 1972. His two sons, Beau and Hunter, though critically injured, survived.

For Joe, meeting Jill meant finding a way forward in the face of tragedy. "She gave me back my life; she made me start to think my family might be whole again," Joe wrote in his 2007 memoir, *Promises to Keep*.[1] Jill, too, had been previously married, finally agreeing to marry Joe in 1977 after five proposals – a story that has often been retold in media coverage of the couple. In 1981, the two had a daughter, Ashley.

Though Jill married a man whose career had been staked in politics, she forged ahead with her lifelong passion for education, earning a master's from both West Chester University in 1981 and Villanova University in 1987. She later returned to her alma mater, the University of Delaware, to earn a doctorate in education in 2007.

Jill's experience in the field is expansive, having taught in the Delaware public school system, at Delaware Technical & Community College, and eventually at Northern Virginia Community College, a position she maintained while second lady.

"I can have my own job, my own life, but also work on issues," she told *People* in 2009, shortly after Joe's election as vice president. "I can have it all, really."[2]

And she did. Between teaching and fulfilling the traditional duties of a second lady, Jill used her newfound platform to advocate for community colleges, which she has repeatedly heralded as one of America's "best kept secrets."[3] In 2010, Jill held the first White House Summit on Community Colleges with President Barack Obama to call attention to the role of community colleges in cultivating the nation's workforce. In 2012, Jill embarked on a three-day Community College to Career bus tour with then-Secretary of Labor Hilda Solis to highlight partnerships between schools and employers.

But Jill's advocacy hasn't been limited to education. The same year, she published a children's book titled *Don't Forget, God Bless Our Troops*, which illustrates the experience of her granddaughter, Natalie, as she watches her father, Beau, being deployed to Iraq.

In 2015, Joe was hit with immense tragedy again when Beau died after a battle against brain cancer. For Jill, who had helped to raise him, the loss was deeply felt. "I am not the same," she wrote in her

2019 memoir, *Where the Light Enters: Building a Family, Discovering Myself*. "I feel it every day. I think every mother who has lost a child must feel this way. Am I able to feel happiness? Yes, definitely. But it's not as pure; there's just not the magic to life I used to feel."[4]

At the 2020 Democratic National Convention where Joe officially accepted his party's nomination for president, he praised Jill as "so damn tough and loyal."[5]

While Jill was active as second lady, according to *The Washington Post*, her involvement on the campaign trail didn't reach its peak until Joe's 2020 run.[6] That reportedly marked the first time she had paused her teaching career since the birth of her daughter nearly four decades prior.[7]

Appearing virtually at the convention – an event that had been shifted to computer and television screens amid the Coronavirus pandemic – Jill gave a heartfelt speech in support of her husband's run from the Brandywine High School classroom in Wilmington where she once taught.

"I know that if we entrust this nation to Joe, he will do for your family what he did for ours – bring us together and make us whole, carry us forward in our time of need, keep the promise of America for all of us," she said.[8]

Having returned to Washington now as first lady, Jill has no intention to set aside her love of teaching, committing to keeping up with her career just as she had before. Making that promise in an interview with *CBS News Sunday Morning*, she said, "It's important, and I want people to value teachers and know their contributions and lift up their profession."[9]

AFTERWORD

BY ANTHONY J EKSTEROWICZ

WHAT WILL IT TAKE TO ELECT THE FIRST FEMALE PRESIDENT OF THE UNITED STATES?

For women, having historically been deprived of the vote for nearly a century and a half, it has been a difficult road. Property and inheritance laws throughout the United States favoured males during the eighteenth and nineteenth centuries. Family duties, religion, and traditional values kept women homebound and largely out of politics. Educational levels and schooling also played a part in impeding women.

First ladies' studies, however, point to significant progress for female influence at the highest levels of the U.S, government structure, illuminating how far women have come in achieving significant influence over public policy. All of this points to hopeful future trends for the election of the first female president.

First ladies have gradually moved from being non-partners in their husband's presidency to being full partners not only in charitable causes but also political matters. We should note the contributions of Edith Wilson, Eleanor Roosevelt, Betty Ford, Hillary Clinton and even Nancy Reagan. First ladies are now considered trusted presidential allies and advisers, dependent upon their relationship with the president and their desire to be assertive in their own right.

The political influence wielded by first ladies depends upon their background, from educational achievement to job experience. Generally the more independent and professional the background the more influence she wields. More independent and activist first ladies will always be controversial. But the handling of controversy provides a breeding ground of experience that can be utilized to seek higher office.

These factors have served to professionalize the Office of the First Lady. Higher-paid staffers with greater educations have worked for the first lady, and an increasing number of her advisers have become presidential advisers, attending morning briefings and working closely with the president's personal staff. This has bridged differences between the west and east wings of the White House and further integrated them in the modern era.

The result has been greater responsibility for policy development. Now, first ladies have the professional tools – an established office – and relationships – advisers integrated into the West Wing – to not only aid in policy development, but oversee policy explanation to Congress. There is one caveat to note: Not every first lady will pursue these ends. In the final analysis, it depends upon her own inclination which, in turn, is affected by a host of variables such as her temperament, family situations and her relationship with the president.

As these trends continue, it would not be unusual for first ladies with large political ambitions to use this office as a stepping stone to future influential positions or political offices. This is certainly what Eleanor Roosevelt did with her work at the founding of the United Nations. It is also the path that Hillary Clinton chose in her successful run for the Senate, two presidential campaigns, and her service as United States Secretary of State.

So where does this leave us concerning the election of the first woman president? Contemporary women seeking political office in our modern era are more highly educated, with larger professional portfolios combined with the ambition to propel them to seek political offices. Many already are serving in influential positions of power. While the pool of potential female presidential candidates is small, it is noticeably growing. As these trends continue we should see a female president relatively soon.

ENDNOTES

INTRODUCTION

1. Adams, A. (1776) *Letter from Abigail Adams to John Adams, 31 March - 5 April 1776* [online]. Massachusetts Historical Society. Available at: https://www.masshist.org/digitaladams/archive/doc?id=L17760331aa [Accessed 8 Jul. 2019].
2. Miller Center. (n.d.) *Sarah Polk* [online]. Available at: https://millercenter.org/president/polk/essays/polk-1845-firstlady [Accessed 6 Aug. 2019].
3. Thomas, L. (2016) *The Melania Trump of the 19th Century* [online]. Politico. Available at: https://www.politico.com/magazine/story/2016/05/melania-trump-19th-century-louisa-adams-first-lady-213908 [Accessed 23 Jul. 2019].
4. C-SPAN. (2013) *First Ladies: Influence and Image* [video]. Available at: https://www.c-span.org/video/?c4386235/lady-dolley-madison [Accessed 16 Jul. 2019].
5. Wilson, E. (1980) *My memoir*. New York: Arno Press, p. 289.

MARTHA DANDRIDGE CUSTIS WASHINGTON

1. Gehred, K. (2016) *John Custis vs. Martha Dandridge* [online]. Washington Papers. Available at: http://gwpapers.virginia.edu/john-custis-vs-martha-dandridge/#_ednref12 [Accessed 6 Jul. 2019].
2. C-SPAN. (2013) *First Ladies: Influence and Image* [video]. Available at: https://www.c-span.org/video/?310724-1/ladies-series [Accessed 5 Jul. 2019].
3. Gehred.
4. Ibid.
5. Ibid.
6. Mount Vernon. (n.d.) *Ten Facts About Martha Washington* [online]. Available at: https://www.mountvernon.org/george-washington/martha-washington/ten-facts-about-martha-washington/ [Accessed 6 Jul. 2019].
7. C-SPAN.
8. Mount Vernon. (n.d.) *Biography of Martha Washington* [online]. Available at: https://www.mountvernon.org/george-washington/martha-washington/biography/ [Accessed 6 Jul. 2019].
9. Ibid.
10. Mount Vernon. (n.d.) *At the Front* [online]. Available at: https://www.mountvernon.org/george-washington/martha-washington/martha-at-the-front/ [Accessed 6 Jul. 2019].
11. C-SPAN.
12. Ibid.
13. Washington, M. (1789) *Letter, Martha Washington to Fanny Bassett Washington, October 23, 1789.* [online] Available at: http://marthawashington.us/items/show/13 [Accessed 6 Jul. 2019].
14. Washington, M. (1789) *Letter, Martha Washington to Mercy Otis Warren, December 26, 1789.* [online] Available at: http://marthawashington.us/items/show/25 [Accessed 6 Jul. 2019].
15. Mount Vernon. (n.d.) *First Lady Martha Washington's Trip to New York* [online]. Available at: https://www.mountvernon.org/george-washington/martha-washington/martha-washingtons-inaugural-trip-to-washington/ [Accessed 5 Jul. 2019].
16. National First Ladies' Library. (n.d.) *First Lady Biography: Martha Washington* [online]. Available at: http://www.firstladies.org/biographies/firstladies.aspx?biography=1 [Accessed 5 Jul. 2019].
17. Ibid.
18. Adams, A. (1789) *Abigail Adams to Mary Smith Cranch, 12 July 1789* [online]. Available

at: https://founders.archives.gov/documents/Adams/04-08-02-0210 [Accessed 8 Jul. 2019].
19. National First Ladies' Library. (n.d.) *First Lady Biography: Martha Washington* [online] . http://www.firstladies.org/biographies/firstladies.aspx?biography=1 [Accessed 8 Jul. 2019].
20. Ibid.
21. Mount Vernon. (n.d.) *The Deaths of George & Martha* [online]. Available at: https://www.mountvernon.org/george-washington/martha-washington/the-deaths-of-george-martha/ [Accessed 6 Sept. 2019].
22. Ibid.
23. Ibid.
24. Glass, A. (2018) *Martha Washington dies, May 21, 1802* [online]. Available at: https://www.politico.com/story/2013/05/lady-washington-died-of-fever-may-21-1802-091693 [Accessed 6 Sept. 2019].
25. Mount Vernon. (n.d.) *Martha on $1* [online]. Available at: https://www.mountvernon.org/george-washington/martha-washington/martha-on-1/#:~:text=Martha%20Washington's%20image%20appears%20on,Certificates%20were%20discontinued%20in%201957 [Accessed 6 Jul. 2019].

ABIGAIL SMITH ADAMS

1. National First Ladies' Library. (n.d.) *First Lady Biography: Abigail Adams* [online]. Available at: http://www.firstladies.org/biographies/firstladies.aspx?biography=2 [Accessed 8 Jul. 2019].
2. Michals, D. (2015) *Abigail Smith Adams* [online]. Available at: https://www.womenshistory.org/education-resources/biographies/abigail-adams [Accessed 8 Jul. 2019].
3. Ibid.
4. Adams, A. (1776) *Letter from Abigail Adams to John Adams, 31 March – 5 April 1776* [online]. Massachusetts Historical Society. Available at: https://www.masshist.org/digitaladams/archive/doc?id=L17760331aa [Accessed 8 Jul. 2019].
5. Adams, A. (1796) *Letter from Abigail Adams to John Adams, 23 December 1796* [online]. Massachusetts Historical Society. Available at: http://www.masshist.org/digitaladams/archive/doc?id=L17961223aa [Accessed 8 Jul. 2019].
6. Adams, A. (1797) *Letter from Abigail Adams to John Adams, 29 January 1797* [online]. Massachusetts Historical Society. Available at: https://www.masshist.org/digitaladams/archive/doc?id=L17970129aa [Accessed 6 Jul. 2019].
7. Adams, A. (1797) *Abigail Adams to Mary Smith Cranch, 6 June 1797* [online]. Available at: https://founders.archives.gov/documents/Adams/04-12-02-0089 [Accessed 8 Jul. 2019].
8. Adams, J. (1797) *Letter from John Adams to Abigail Adams, 22 March 1797* [online]. Available at: http://www.masshist.org/digitaladams/archive/doc?id=L17970322ja
9. Miller Center. (2016) *Abigail Adams* [online]. Available at: https://millercenter.org/president/adams/adams-1797-abigail-firstlady [Accessed 8 Jul. 2019].
10. Ibid.
11. Ibid.
12. Ibid.
13. Ibid.
14. Roberts, J. (2004) *Rating The First Ladies: The Women Who Influenced The Presidency*. New York: Citadel Press, p. 17.

15. Ibid.
16. History, (n.d.) *John Adams moves into White House* [online]. https://www.history.com/this-day-in-history/john-adams-moves-into-white-house [Accessed 8 Jul. 2019].
17. Ibid.
18. Ibid.

MARTHA WAYLES SKELTON JEFFERSON

1. National First Ladies' Library. (n.d.) *First Lady Biography: Martha Jefferson* [online]. Available at: http://www.firstladies.org/biographies/firstladies.aspx?biography=3 [Accessed 12 Jul. 2019].
2. Wilson, G. (1998) *Martha Wayles Skelton Jefferson.* [online] Available at: https://www.monticello.org/site/research-and-collections/martha-wayles-skelton-jefferson [Accessed 12 Jul. 2019].
3. Ibid.
4. Jefferson, M. (1782) *Lines Copied from Tristram Shandy by Martha and Thomas Jefferson* [online]. Available at: https://founders.archives.gov/documents/Jefferson/01-06-02-0185 [Accessed 13 Jul. 2019].
5. Wilson.
6. Jefferson, M. (1782) *From Thomas Jefferson to Chastellux, 26 November 1782* [online]. Available at: https://founders.archives.gov/documents/Jefferson/01-06-02-0192 [Accessed 13 Jul. 2019].
7. Klapthor, M. and Black, A. (2006) *The First Ladies of the United States of America*. Washington: White House Historical Association, p. 13.
8. Jefferson, M. (1782) *From Thomas Jefferson to Chastellux, 26 November 1782.*
9. Coolidge, E. (1856). *Extract from Ellen W. Randolph Coolidge to Henry S. Randall* [online]. Available at: http://tjrs.monticello.org/letter/1986 [Accessed 13 Jul. 2019].
10. Jefferson, M. (1782) *From Thomas Jefferson to Chastellux, 26 November 1782.*
11. National First Ladies' Library.
12. C-SPAN. (2013) *First Ladies: Influence and Image* [video]. Available at: http://firstladies.c-span.org/FirstLady/4/Martha-Jefferson.aspx [Accessed 13 Jul. 2019].

DOLLEY PAYNE TODD MADISON

1. Montpelier. (n.d.) *Becoming America's First Lady* [online]. Available at: https://www.montpelier.org/learn/dolley-madison-becoming-americas-first-lady [Accessed 15 Jul. 2019].
2. Ibid.
3. Ibid.
4. Ibid.
5. Scofield, M. (2012) *Unraveling the Dolley Myths* [online]. Available at: https://www.whitehousehistory.org/unraveling-the-dolley-myths [Accessed 16 Jul. 2019].
6. Montpelier.
7. Virginia Center for Digital History. (n.d.) *The Washington Years: 1801-1817* [online]. Available at: http://www2.vcdh.virginia.edu/madison/overview/wash.html [Accessed 15 Jul. 2019].
8. Ibid.
9. Gould, L. (2001) *American First Ladies: Their Lives and Their Legacy*, 2nd ed. London: Routledge, p. 29.
10. Montpelier.
11. Ibid.
12. Ibid.
13. C-SPAN. (2013) *First Ladies: Influence and Image*

[video]. Available at: https://www.c-span.org/video/?c4386235/lady-dolley-madison [Accessed 16 Jul. 2019].

14. Montpelier.

15. Daily National Intelligencer. (1849) *Funeral of Mrs. Madison* [online]. Available at: http://www2.vcdh.virginia.edu/madison/exhibit/widowhood/img/art2.html [Accessed 16 Jul. 2019].

16. National Park Service. (2017) *Summer 1814: Dolley Madison saves Washington's portrait, with some help* [online]. Available at: https://www.nps.gov/articles/dolley-madison-washingtons-portrait.htm [Accessed 16 Jul. 2019].

17. Ibid.

18. Ibid.

19. Madison, D. (1814) *Letter from Dolley Madison to Lucy Todd* [online]. Available at: https://www.encyclopediavirginia.org/Letter_from_Dolley_Madison_to_Lucy_Todd_August_23_1814 [Accessed 17 Jul. 2019].

20. North Carolina Museum of History. (n.d.) *Dolly's Legends* [online]. Available at: https://www.ncmuseumofhistory.org/dollys-legends [Accessed 16 Jul. 2019].

21. Madison, D. (1848) *Letter from Dolley Madison to Robert G. L. De Peyster* [online]. Available at: https://www.encyclopediavirginia.org/Letter_from_Dolley_Madison_to_Robert_G_L_De_Peyster_February_11_1848 [Accessed 16 Jul. 2019].

ELIZABETH KORTRIGHT MONROE

1. Miller Center. (n.d.) *Elizabeth Monroe* [online]. Available at: https://millercenter.org/president/monroe/essays/monroe-1817-firstlady [Accessed 19 Jul. 2019].

2. C-SPAN. (2013) *First Ladies: Influence and Image* [video]. Available at: https://www.c-span.org/video/?c4391380/elizabeth-monroe-program [Accessed 19 Jul. 2019].

3. Miller Center.

4. National First Ladies' Library. (n.d.) *First Lady Biography: Elizabeth Monroe* [online]. Available at: http://www.firstladies.org/biographies/firstladies.aspx?biography=5 [Accessed 19 Jul. 2019].

5. Gould, L. (2001). *American First Ladies: Their Lives and Their Legacy*, 2nd ed. London: Routledge, p.39.

6. National First Ladies' Library.

7. Ibid.

8. Ibid.

9. C-SPAN.

10. Miller Center.

11. C-SPAN.

12. Harris, S. and Kearney, J. (2014) *Articles of the Best Kind* [online]. Available at: https://www.whitehousehistory.org/articles-of-the-best-kind [Accessed 6 Sept. 2019].

13. National First Ladies' Library.

LOUISA CATHERINE JOHNSON ADAMS

1. Thomas, L. (2016) *Louisa: The Extraordinary Life of Mrs. Adams*. New York: Penguin Books, p. 5.

2. National Park Service. (2017) *Louisa Catherine Adams* [online]. Available at: https://www.nps.gov/adam/learn/historyculture/louisa-catherine-adams-1775-1852.htm [Accessed 24 Jul. 2019].

3. Mansky, J. (2016) *Meet the First and Only Foreign-Born First Lady: Louisa Catherine Adams* [online]. Available at: https://www.smithsonianmag.com/history/meet-the-first-and-only-foreign-born-first-lady-louisa-cathernine-adams-180959149/ [Accessed 23 Jul. 2019].

4. Ibid.

5. Thomas, p. 258.

6. Mansky.

7. National Park Service.

8. Thomas, L. (2016) *The Melania Trump of the 19th Century*. [online] Available at: https://www.politico.com/magazine/story/2016/05/melania-trump-19th-century-louisa-adams-first-lady-213908 [Accessed 23 Jul. 2019].

9. Ibid.

10. Mansky.

11. Blakemore, E. (2016). *'Melania Trump Won't Be America's First Foreign-Born First Lady'* [online] JSTOR. Available at: https://daily.jstor.org/melania-trump-wont-be-americas-first-foreign-born-first-lady/ [Accessed 23 Jul. 2019].

12. Thomas, L. (2016). *The Melania Trump of the 19th Century*.

13. Ibid.

14. Ibid.

15. Ibid.

16. Ibid.

17. Ibid.

RACHEL DONELSON JACKSON

1. Owsley, H. (1977) *'The Marriages of Rachel Donelson'*, *Tennessee Historical Quarterly, Volume* (36) 4, p. 481 [online]. Available at: https://www.jstor.org/stable/42625784 [Accessed 24 Jul. 2019].

2. Toplovich, A. (2017) *'This is the Real Story of Andrew and Rachel Jackson'*, *Tennessean* [online]. Available at: https://www.tennessean.com/story/opinion/2017/05/05/real-story-andrew-and-rachel-jackson/101194482/ [Accessed 23 Jul. 2019].

3. Boissoneault, L. (2017) *Rachel Jackson, the Scandalous Divorcee Who Almost Became First Lady* [online]. Available at: https://www.smithsonianmag.com/history/rachel-jackson-was-original-monica-lewinsky-180963713/ [Accessed 23 Jul. 2019].

4. Owsley, p. 491.

5. Ibid.

6. Ibid, p. 479.

7. Miller Center. (n.d.) *Emily Donelson, Sarah Jackson* [online]. Available at: https://millercenter.org/president/jackson/essays/jackson-1829-firstlady [Accessed 23 Jul. 2019].

8. Ibid.

9. Wilcox, E. (1898). 'Andrew Jackson: His Life, Times and Compatriots.' *Frank Leslie's Popular Monthly*, (46), p. 148.

10. Boissoneault.

HANNAH HOES VAN BUREN

1. Bradley, J. (n.d.) 'Hannah Hoes Van Buren, Part I', *The Papers of Martin Van Buren* [online]. Available at: http://vanburenpapers.org/content/hannah-van-buren-part-i [Accessed 29 Jul. 2019].

2. Ibid.

3. White House Historical Association. (n.d.) *Hannah Van Buren* [online]. Available at: https://www.whitehousehistory.org/bios/hannah-van-buren [Accessed 29 Jul. 2019].

4. National First Ladies' Library. (n.d.) *First Lady Biography: Hannah Van Buren* [online]. Available at: http://www.firstladies.org/biographies/firstladies.aspx?biography=8 [Accessed 29 Jul. 2019].

5. Holloway, L. (1881) *Ladies of the White House; Or, In the Home of the Presidents*. Philadelphia: Bradley & Company, p. 336.

6. Ibid, p. 337.

7. Ibid.

8. Ibid.

9. Ibid.

ANNA TUTHILL SYMMES HARRISON

1. C-SPAN. (2013) *First Ladies: Influence and Image* [video]. Available at: https://www.c-span.org/video/?310730-1/ladies-anna-harrison-letitia-tyler-julia-tyler [Accessed 30 Jul. 2019].

2. Ibid.

3. White House Historical Association. (n.d.) *Anna Harrison* [online]. Available at: https://www.whitehousehistory.org/bios/anna-harrison [Accessed 29 Jul. 2019].

4. C-SPAN.

5. Ibid.

LETITIA CHRISTIAN TYLER

1. Leahy, C. (2006) 'Torn between Family and Politics: John Tyler's Struggle for Balance', *The Virginia Magazine of History and Biography*, Volume 114(3), p. 324 [online]. Available at: https://www.jstor.org/stable/4250328 [Accessed 30 Jul. 2019].

2. Ibid.

3. C-SPAN. (2013) *First Ladies: Influence and Image* [video]. Available at: https://www.c-span.org/video/?310730-1/ladies-anna-harrison-letitia-tyler-julia-tyler [Accessed 30 Jul. 2019].

4. Graddy, L. and Pastan, A. (2014). *The Smithsonian First Ladies Collection*. Washington, D.C.: Smithsonian Institution, p. 82.

5. Holloway, L. (1881) *Ladies of the White House; Or, In the Home of the Presidents*. Philadelphia: Bradley & Company, p. 384.

6. Ibid.

7. C-SPAN.

JULIA GARDINER TYLER

1. National First Ladies' Library. (n.d.) *First Lady Biography: Julia Tyler*. [online] Available at: http://www.firstladies.org/biographies/firstladies.aspx?biography=11 [Accessed 2 Aug. 2019].

2. Glass, A. (2018) *John Tyler becomes first president to wed while in office, June 26,1844* [online]. Available at: https://www.politico.com/story/2018/06/26/john-tyler-becomes-first-president-to-wed-while-in-office-june-26-664821 [Accessed 30 Jul. 2019].

3. Fremont, J. (1887) *Souvenirs of My Time*. Boston: D. Lothrop and Company, pp. 99–100.

4. Ibid.

5. Ibid.

6. Library of Congress. (n.d.) *Hail to the Chief* [online]. Available at: https://www.loc.gov/item/ihas.200000009/ [Accessed 2 Aug. 2019].

7. National First Ladies' Library.

8. Ibid.

9. Roberts, B. (2004) *Rating The First Ladies: The Women Who Influenced The Presidency*. New York: Citadel Press Books, p. 66.

10. National First Ladies' Library.

11. Ibid.

12. Hendricks, N. (2015) *America's First Ladies: A Historical Encyclopedia and Primary Document Collection of the Remarkable Women of the White House*. Santa Barbara: ABC-CLIO, p. 80.

13. Ibid.

14. Miller Center. (n.d.) *Julia Gardiner Tyler* [online]. Available at: https://millercenter.org/president/tyler/essays/tyler-julia-1841-firstlady [Accessed 2 Aug. 2019].

15. Adler, B. (2006) *America's First Ladies: Their Uncommon Wisdom, From Martha Washington to Laura Bush*. Lanham: Taylor Trade Publishing, p. 35.

16. Beasley, M. (2005) *First ladies and the press: the unfinished partnership of the media age*. Evanston: Northwestern University Press, p. 40.

17. Ibid.

18. Ibid.

SARAH CHILDRESS POLK

1. Diamond, A. (2019) *How First Lady Sarah Polk*

Set a Model for Conservative Female Power [online]. Smithsonian.com. Available at: https://www.smithsonianmag.com/history/how-first-lady-sarah-polk-set-model-conservative-female-power-180971393/ [Accessed 6 Aug. 2019].

2. Caroli, B. (2010) *First Ladies: From Martha Washington to Michelle Obama.* New York: Oxford University Press, p. 61.

3. Ibid, pp. 61-62.

4. Beasley, M. (2005) *First ladies and the press: the unfinished partnership of the media age.* Evanston: Northwestern University Press, p. 41.

5. Nelson, A. and Nelson, F. (1892) *Memorials of Sarah Childress Polk.* New York: Anson D.F. Randolph & Company, p. 93.

6. Miller Center. (n.d.) *Sarah Polk.* [online] Available at: https://millercenter.org/president/polk/essays/polk-1845-firstlady [Accessed 6 Aug. 2019].

7. Diamond.

8. Ibid.

9. Greenberg, A. (2013) *A Wicked War: Polk, Clay, Lincoln, and the 1846 U.S. Invasion of Mexico.* New York: Vintage Books, p. 72.

10. Diamond.

11. Miller Center.

12. Greenberg, A. (2019) *Lady First: The World of Mrs. James K. Polk.* New York: Alfred A. Knopf, p. xxiii.

13. Ibid.

MARGARET MACKALL SMITH TAYLOR

1. Thacker-Estrada, E. (2006) 'True Women.' In: R. Watson and A. Eksterowicz, eds., *The Presidential Companion: Readings on the First Ladies,* 2nd ed. Columbia: University of South Carolina Press, p. 78.

2. Mayo, P. (1996) *The Smithsonian Book of the First Ladies: Their Lives, Times, and Issues.* New York: Henry Holt and Company, p. 76.

3. Ibid.

4. Caroli, B. (2010) *First Ladies: From Martha Washington to Michelle Obama.* 4th ed. New York: Oxford University Press, p.49.

5. Ibid.

6. Ibid, p. 79.

7. Beasley, M. (2005) *First ladies and the press: the unfinished partnership of the media age.* Evanston: Northwestern University Press, p. 41.

8. Taylor, Z. (1908) *Letters of Zachary Taylor From the Battle-Fields of the Mexican War.* Rochester: The Genesee Press, p. x.

9. Thacker-Estrada, p. 90.

10. Thacker-Estrada, p. 91.

11. Caroli.

12. National First Ladies' Library (n.d.). *First Lady Biography: Margaret Taylor* [online]. Available at: http://www.firstladies.org/biographies/firstladies.aspx?biography=13 [Accessed 6 Aug. 2019].

13. Ibid.

ABIGAIL POWERS FILLMORE

1. Thacker-Estrada, E. (2006) 'True Women', in Watson R. and Eksterowicz A. (eds.) *The Presidential Companion: Readings on the First Ladies,* 2nd ed. Columbia: University of South Carolina Press, p. 91.

2. Thacker-Estrada, E. (2001) 'The Heart of the Fillmore Presidency: Abigail Powers Fillmore and the White House Library', *White House Studies,* Volume 1(1) [online]. Available at: https://go.gale.com/ps/anonymous?id=GALE%7CA80605884 [Accessed 6 Aug., 2019].

3. Rayback, R. (2017). *Millard Fillmore: Biography Of A President.* [s.n.] p. 19.

4. Thacker-Estrada, E. (2001).

5. Caroli, B. (2010) *First Ladies: From Martha Washington to Michelle Obama.* 4th ed. New York: Oxford University Press, p. 49.

6. Caroli, p. 52.

7. Caroli, p. 50.

8. Severance, F. (1907) *Millard Fillmore Papers.* Buffalo: Buffalo Historical Society, p. 489.

9. Deppisch, L. (2015) *The Health of the First Ladies: Medical Histories from Martha Washington to Michelle Obama.* Jefferson: McFarland & Company p. 50.

JANE APPLETON PIERCE

1. Deppisch, L. (2015) *The Health of the First Ladies: Medical Histories from Martha Washington to Michelle Obama.* Jefferson: McFarland & Company, p. 57.

2. Nichols, R. (1993) *Franklin Pierce: Young Hickory of the Granite Hills.* Newtown: American Political Biography Press, p. 76.

3. Ibid.

4. Ibid.

5. Thacker-Estrada, E. (2006) 'True Women' in Watson R. and Eksterowicz A. (eds.) *The Presidential Companion: Readings on the First Ladies,* 2nd ed. Columbia: University of South Carolina Press, p. 93.

6. Ibid.

7. Caroli, B. (2010) *First Ladies: From Martha Washington to Michelle Obama.* 4th ed. New York: Oxford University Press, p. 54.

8. Ibid.

9. Watson, P. (2004) *Life in the White House: A Social History of the First Family and the President's House.* Albany: State University of New York Press, p. 175.

10. Thacker-Estrada.

11. Deppisch.

12. Thacker-Estrada, p. 94.

13. Miller Center. (n.d.) *Jane Pierce.* [online] Available at: https://millercenter.org/president/pierce/essays/pierce-1853-firstlady [Accessed 20 Aug. 2019].

14. Ibid.

15. Deppisch.

16. Watson, p. 177.

17. Ibid.

18. Deppisch, p. 54.

19. Fuller. (1853) 'Further Particulars of the Accident on the Boston and Maine Railroad – Letter of Rev. Mr. Fuller', *New-York Daily Times* [online]. Available at: https://newspaperarchive.com/new-york-daily-times-jan-10-1853-p-2/ [Accessed 20 Aug. 2019].

20. Ibid.

21. Ibid.

22. Miller Center.

23. Thacker-Estrada, p. 95.

24. Pierce, J. (1853) 'Letter from Jane Means (Appleton) Pierce to her deceased son, Benjamin Pierce, 1853 January 30' [letter]. Available at: https://www.nhhistory.org/object/286351/letter-from-jane-means-appleton-pierce-to-her-deceased-son-benjamin-pierce-1853-january-30 [Accessed 20 Aug. 2019].

25. Miller Center.

26. Ibid.

27. Ibid.

28. Abbott, K. (2012) 'The Fox Sisters and the Rap on Spiritualism', *Smithsonian Magazine* [online]. Available at: https://www.smithsonianmag.com/history/the-fox-sisters-and-the-rap-on-spiritualism-99663697/ [Accessed 20 Aug. 2019].

29. Anthony, C. (2014) *First Ladies & the Occult: Seances and Spiritualists,* Part 1 [online]. Available at: http://www.firstladies.org/blog/first-ladies-the-occult-seances-and-spiritualists-part-1/ [Accessed 20 Aug. 2019].

30. Abbott.

HARRIET REBECCA LANE JOHNSTON

1. Cooper, W. (n.d.) *James Buchanan: Life Before the Presidency* [online]. Available at: https://millercenter.org/president/buchanan/life-before-the-presidency [Accessed 22 Aug. 2019].

2. Mayo, P. (1996) *The Smithsonian Book of the First Ladies: Their Lives, Times, and Issues.* New York: Henry Holt and Company, p. 85.

3. Mrs. Logan, J. (1901) *Thirty Years in Washington; Or, Life and Scenes in Our National Capital.* Hartford: A.D. Worthington & Company, p. 641.

4. Ibid.

5. Caroli, B. (2010) *First Ladies: From Martha Washington to Michelle Obama.* 4th ed. New York: Oxford University Press, p. 43.

6. Blumenthal, S. (2019) *All the Powers of Earth: The Political Life of Abraham Lincoln.* New York: Simon & Schuster, p. 291.

7. Ibid.

8. Caroli, p. 43.

9. Ibid.

10. C-SPAN. (2013) First Ladies: Influence and Image [video]. Available at: https://www.c-span.org/video/?310732-1/ladies-jane-pierce-harriet-lane [Accessed 22 Aug. 2019].

11. Rosenberger, H. (1966) 'Harriet Lane, First Lady: Hostess Extraordinary in Difficult Times', *Records of the Columbia Historical Society,* Volume 66, p. 130 [online]. Available at: https://www.jstor.org/stable/40067251 [Accessed 22 Aug. 2019].

12. Slevin, M. (2019) *Harriet Lane Johnston: First Lady of the National Collection of Fine Arts* [online]. Available at: https://siarchives.si.edu/blog/harriet-lane-johnston-first-lady-national-collection-fine-arts [Accessed 22 Aug. 2019].

13. Ibid.

14. Ibid.

MARY TODD LINCOLN

1. Burlingame, M. (1994) *The Inner World of Abraham Lincoln.* Chicago: University of Illinois Press, p. 297.

2. Caroli, B. (2010) *First Ladies: From Martha Washington to Michelle Obama.* 4th ed. New York: Oxford University Press, p. 71.

3. Ibid.

4. Egerton, D. (2015) *A Matter of Profound Wonder: The Marriage of Abraham Lincoln and Mary Todd.* [online] Available at: http://werehistory.org/mary-todd/ [Accessed 4 Sept. 2019].

5. Blumenthal, S. (2016) *A Self-Made Man: The Political Life of Abraham Lincoln.* New York: Simon & Schuster, p. 276.

6. Ibid.

7. Ibid.

8. Miller Center. (n.d.) *Mary Lincoln.* [online] Available at: https://millercenter.org/president/lincoln/essays/lincoln-1861-firstlady [Accessed 4 Sept. 2019].

9. Baker, J. (1989) *Mary Todd Lincoln: A Biography.* New York: W.W. Norton & Company, p. 161.

10. Ibid, p. 162.

11. Caroli, p. 73.

12. Ibid.

13. Emerson, J. (2007) *The Madness of Mary Lincoln.* Carbondale: Southern Illinois University Press, p. 13.

14. Caroli, p. 75.

15. Caroli, p. 74.

16. Ibid.

17. Burlingame.

18. Caroli, p. 76.

19. Caroli, p. 77.

20. Caroli, p. 78.

21. Caroli, p. 77.

22. Caroli, pp. 78-79.

ELIZA MCCARDLE JOHNSON

1. Hendricks, N. (2015) *America's First Ladies: A Historical Encyclopedia and Primary Document Collection*

of the Remarkable Women of the White House. Santa Barbara: ABC-CLIO, p. 134.
2. C-SPAN. (2013) First Ladies: Influence and Image [video]. Available at: https://www.c-span.org/video/?310734-1/lady-eliza-johnson [Accessed 18 Sept. 2019].
3. Ibid.
4. National First Ladies' Library. (n.d.) First Lady Biography: Eliza Johnson. [online] Available at: http://www.firstladies.org/biographies/firstladies.aspx?biography=18 [Accessed 18 Sept. 2019].
5. Ibid.
6. Deppisch, L. (2015) The Health of the First Ladies: Medical Histories from Martha Washington to Michelle Obama. Jefferson: McFarland & Company, p. 83.
7. White House Historical Association. (n.d.). Eliza Johnson [online] Available at: https://www.whitehousehistory.org/bios/eliza-johnson [Accessed 29 Sept. 2019].
8. Lockwood, M. (1915) Yesterdays in Washington. Rosslyn: The Commonwealth Company, p. 281.
9. Ibid.
10. Moore, M. (1893) 'The Daughter of Andrew Johnson', The Ladies' Home Journal, (10), p. 5.
11. Ibid.
12. Caroli, B. (2010) First Ladies: From Martha Washington to Michelle Obama. 4th ed. New York: Oxford University Press, p. 57.
13. C-SPAN.
14. Hendricks, p. 139.
15. Miller Center. (n.d.) Eliza Johnson, Martha Johnson. [online] Available at: https://millercenter.org/president/johnson/essays/johnson-1865-firstlady [Accessed 18 Sept. 2019].
16. Ibid.
17. C-SPAN.
18. Hendricks.
19. Hendricks, pp. 141-142.
20. Ibid.
21. Miller Center.

JULIA DENT GRANT

1. C-SPAN. (2013) First Ladies: Influence and Image [video]. Available at: https://www.c-span.org/video/?310735-1/lady-julia-grant [Accessed 25 Sept. 2019].
2. Roberts, J. (2004) Rating The First Ladies: The Women Who Influenced The Presidency. Citadel Press, p. 126.
3. Roberts, p. 127.
4. King, G. (2012) General Grant in Love and War [online]. Available at: https://www.smithsonianmag.com/history/general-grant-in-love-and-war-94609512/ [Accessed 25 Sept. 2019].
5. Roberts.
6. Roberts, p. 128.
7. Roberts, p. 126.
8. Caroli, B. (2010) First Ladies: From Martha Washington to Michelle Obama. 4th ed. New York: Oxford University Press, p. 82.
9. Beasley, M. (2005) First ladies and the press: the unfinished partnership of the media age. Evanston: Northwestern University Press, p. 45.
10. Caroli.
11. Ibid.
12. Ibid.
13. Grant, J. (1975) The Personal Memoirs of Julia Dent Grant. Carbondale: Southern Illinois University Press, p. 183.
14. Beasley.
15. Caroli, p. 83.
16. Ibid.
17. Caroli, p. 84.
18. Grant, p. 182.

LUCY WARE WEBB HAYES

1. Hendricks, N. (2015) America's First Ladies: A Historical Encyclopedia and Primary Document Collection of the Remarkable Women of the White House. Santa Barbara: ABC-CLIO, p. 151.
2. Geer, E. (n.d.) Lucy Webb Hayes and Her Influence Upon Her Era. [online] Available at: https://www.rbhayes.org/hayes/lucy-webb-hayes-and-her-influence-upon-her-era/ [Accessed 3 Oct. 2019].
3. Ibid.
4. Ibid.
5. Caroli, B. (2010) First Ladies: From Martha Washington to Michelle Obama. 4th ed. New York: Oxford University Press, p. 89.
6. Hendricks, p. 152.
7. Ibid.
8. Hoogenboom, A. (n.d.) Rutherford B. Hayes: Campaigns and Elections [online]. Available at: https://millercenter.org/president/hayes/campaigns-and-elections [Accessed 3 Oct. 2019].
9. Holloway, L. (1881) Ladies of the White House: Or, In the Home of the Presidents. Philadelphia: Bradley & Company, p. 655.
10. Caroli, p. 88.
11. Gould, L. (2001) American First Ladies: Their Lives and Their Legacy. 2nd ed. London: Routledge, p. 151.
12. Ibid.
13. Caroli, p. 93.
14. Caroli, p. 92.
15. Caroli, p. 90.

LUCRETIA RUDOLPH GARFIELD

1. Tucker, N. (2019) The Love Letters of James and Lucretia Garfield [online]. Available at: https://blogs.loc.gov/loc/2019/08/now-online-the-love-letters-of-james-and-lucretia-garfield/ [Accessed 6 Oct. 2019]
2. Ibid.
3. Caroli, B. (2010) First Ladies: From Martha Washington to Michelle Obama. 4th ed. New York: Oxford University Press, p. 97.
4. Caroli, p. 98.
5. Shaw, J. (1994) Crete and James: Personal Letters of Lucretia and James Garfield. East Lansing: Michigan State University Press, p. 99.
6. Caroli, p. 99.
7. Ibid.
8. Shaw, p. 104.
9. Ibid.
10. Rutkow, I. (2006) James A. Garfield: The American Presidents Series. New York: Times Books, p. 56.
11. Shaw, J. (2004) Lucretia. New York: Nova History Publishers, Inc. p. 96.
12. Ibid.
13. Caroli, pp. 101–102.
14. Caroli, p. 101.
15. Ibid.
16. National First Ladies' Library (n.d.). First Lady Biography: Lucretia Garfield [online]. Available at: http://www.firstladies.org/biographies/firstladies.aspx?biography=21 [Accessed 6 Oct. 2019].

ELLEN LEWIS HERNDON ARTHUR

1. Roberts, J. (2004) Rating The First Ladies: The Women Who Influenced The Presidency. Citadel Press, p. 151.
2. Ibid.
3. Miller Center (n.d.). Mary McElroy [online]. Available at: https://millercenter.org/president/arthur/essays/mcelroy-1881-firstlady [Accessed 9 Oct. 2019].
4. Ibid.
5. Ibid.
6. Ibid.
7. National First Ladies' Library (n.d.). First Lady Biography: Ellen Arthur [online]. Available at: http://www.firstladies.org/biographies/firstladies.

aspx?biography=22 [Accessed 9 Oct. 2019].
8. Ibid.
9. Ibid.

FRANCES FOLSOM CLEVELAND

1. Ackerman, S. (2014) 'The first celebrity first lady: Frances Cleveland', The Washington Post [online]. Available at: https://www.washingtonpost.com/lifestyle/magazine/the-first-celebrity-first-lady-frances-cleveland/2014/06/27/a4a9bdf4-dd4b-11e3-bda1-9b46b2066796_story.html [Accessed 10 Oct. 2019]
2. Beasley, M. (2005) First Ladies and the Press: The Unfinished Partnership of the Media Age. Evanston: Northwestern University Press, p. 47.
3. Ibid.
4. Ibid.
5. Caroli, B. (2010) First Ladies: From Martha Washington to Michelle Obama. 4th ed. New York: Oxford University Press, p. 107.
6. Ibid.
7. McElroy, R. (1923) Grover Cleveland, the Man and the Statesman: An Authorized Biography. New York: Harper & Brothers, p. 286.
8. Dunlap, A. (2009) Frank: The Story of Frances Folsom Cleveland, America's Youngest First Lady. Albany: State University of New York Press, p. 59.
9. Dunlap, p. 42.
10. Ibid.
11. Beasley, p. 48.
12. Dunlap.
13. Brodsky, A. (2000) Grover Cleveland: A Study in Character. New York: Truman Talley Books, p. 175.
14. Caroli, B. (2010) First Ladies: From Martha Washington to Michelle Obama. 4th ed. New York: Oxford University Press, p. 106.

CAROLINE LAVINIA SCOTT HARRISON

1. Caroli, B. (2010) First Ladies: From Martha Washington to Michelle Obama. 4th ed. New York: Oxford University Press, p. 108.
2. Deppisch, L. (2015) The Health of the First Ladies: Medical Histories from Martha Washington to Michelle Obama. Jefferson: McFarland & Company, p. 77.
3. White House Historical Association. (n.d.) Caroline Harrison [online]. Available at: https://www.whitehousehistory.org/bios/caroline-harrison [Accessed 16 Oct. 2019].
4. Miller Center. (n.d.) Caroline Harrison [online]. Available at: https://millercenter.org/president/bharrison/essays/harrison-1889-caroline-firstlady [Accessed 16 Oct. 2019].
5. Ibid.
6. Sibley, K. (2016) A Companion to First Ladies. Malden: John Wiley & Sons, p. 273.
7. Ibid.
8. The White House Museum. (n.d.) Victorian Ornamentation: 1873–1901 [online]. Available at: http://www.whitehousemuseum.org/special/renovation-1873.htm [Accessed 16 Oct. 2019].
9. Swain, S. (2016) First Ladies: Presidential Historians on the Lives of 45 Iconic American Women. New York: PublicAffairs, p. 194.
10. Swain, p. 195.
11. Swain, p. 197.
12. Indiana Historical Bureau (n.d.). First Lady Caroline Harrison [online]. Available at: https://www.in.gov/history/markers/4390.htm [Accessed 16 Oct. 2019].
13. Ibid.

IDA SAXTON MCKINLEY

1. National First Ladies' Library, (n.d.) First Lady Biography: Ida McKinley. [online] Available at: http://www.firstladies.org/biographies/firstladies.

aspx?biography=25 [Accessed 17 Oct. 2019].

2. Ibid.

3. Swain, S. (2016) *First Ladies: Presidential Historians on the Lives of 45 Iconic American Women.* New York: PublicAffairs, p. 203.

4. Ibid.

5. Ibid.

6. Deppisch, L. (2015). *The Health of the First Ladies: Medical Histories from Martha Washington to Michelle Obama.* Jefferson: McFarland & Company, p. 88.

7. Anthony, C. (2013). *Ida McKinley: The Turn-of-the-Century First Lady through War, Assassination, and Secret Disability.* Kent: The Kent State University Press, p. 137.

8. Black, A. (2009). *Ida Saxton McKinley.* [online] White House Historical Association. Available at: https://www.whitehouse.gov/about-the-white-house/first-ladies/ida-saxton-mckinley/ [Accessed 17 Oct. 2019].

9. National First Ladies' Library.

10. Ibid.

11. Swain, p. 206.

12. Beer, T. (1929) *Hanna.* New York: Alfred A. Knopf, p. 103.

13. Anthony, p. 126.

14. Anon. (1901) 'Critical Point is Fast Coming for the President', *The Atlanta Constitution,* p. 3 [online]. Available at: https://www.newspapers.com/newspage/26869310/ [Accessed 23 Oct. 2019].

15. Ibid.

16. Caroli, B. (2010) *First Ladies: From Martha Washington to Michelle Obama.* 4th ed. New York: Oxford University Press, p. 114.

17. Swain, p. 210.

18. National First Ladies' Library.

19. National Park Service. (2019). *Leaving a Legacy.* [online] Available at: https://www.nps.gov/fila/saxton-mckinley-house.htm [Accessed 17 Oct. 2019].

20. National First Ladies' Library.

21. Anthony, p. 138.

22. Ibid.

EDITH KERMIT CAROW ROOSEVELT

1. Theodore Roosevelt Center. (n.d.) *Roosevelt, Edith Kermit Carow.* [online] Available at: https://www.theodorerooseveltcenter.org/Learn-About-TR/TR-Encyclopedia/Family-and-Friends/Edith-Kermit-Carow-Roosevelt.aspx [Accessed 24 Oct. 2019].

2. Ruane, M. (2018) 'A glimpse into the heartache and high jinks in Theodore Roosevelt's life', *The Washington Post* [online]. Available at: https://www.washingtonpost.com/history/2018/10/18/glimpse-into-heartache-hijinks-life-president-theodore-roosevelt/ [Accessed 24 Oct. 2019].

3. Caroli, B. (2010) *First Ladies: From Martha Washington to Michelle Obama.* 4th ed. New York: Oxford University Press, p. 122.

4. Gould, L. (1987) *Modern First Ladies: An Institutional Perspective.* Prologue: *The Journal of the National Archives,* 19(1), p. 73.

5. Theodore Roosevelt Center.

6. Swain, S. (2016) *First Ladies: Presidential Historians on the Lives of 45 Iconic American Women.* New York: PublicAffairs, p. 217.

7. Damon, A. (1974) *A Look at the Record: Presidential Expenses.* [online] Available at: https://www.americanheritage.com/presidential-expenses [Accessed 23 Oct. 2019].

8. Black, A. (2001) 'The Modern First Lady and Public Policy: From Edith Wilson Through Hillary Rodham Clinton', *OAH Magazine of History,* 15(3), p. 15 [online]. Available at: https://www.jstor.org/stable/25163436 [Accessed 23 Oct. 2019].

9. Gould, L. (2001) *American First Ladies: Their Lives and Their Legacy.* 2nd ed. London: Routledge, p. 206.

10. Caroli, p. 124.

11. Caroli, pp. 122–23.

12. Ruane.

13. Ibid.

HELEN HERRON TAFT

1. Taft, H. (1914) *Recollections of Full Years.* New York: Dodd, Mead & Company, p. 10.

2. Ibid, p. 11.

3. Colman, E. (1927) *White House Gossip: from Andrew Johnson to Calvin Coolidge,* Garden City: Doubleday, Page & Company, p. 323.

4. Gould, L. (2001) *American First Ladies: Their Lives and Their Legacy.* 2nd ed. London: Routledge, p. 7.

5. Caroli, B. (2010) *First Ladies: From Martha Washington to Michelle Obama.* 4th ed. New York: Oxford University Press, p. 128.

6. Gould, p. 14.

7. Ibid.

8. Colman, pp. 326–27.

9. Ibid.

10. Caroli, p. 130.

11. Morison, E. (1952) *The Letters of Theodore Roosevelt: Volume 5, The Big Stick.* Cambridge: Harvard University Press, p. 183.

12. White House Historical Association, (n.d.). *William Howard Taft.* [online] Available at: https://www.whitehouse.gov/about-the-white-house/presidents/william-howard-taft/ [Accessed 24 Oct. 2019].

13. Deppisch, L. (2015) *The Health of the First Ladies: Medical Histories from Martha Washington to Michelle Obama.* Jefferson: McFarland & Company, p. 99.

14. National Park Service, (n.d.). *New Beginnings: Cherry Blossoms and Helen Taft's Landscape Diplomacy.* [online] Available at: https://www.nps.gov/articles/new-beginnings-cherry-blossoms-helen-taft.htm [Accessed 24 Oct. 2019].

15. Colman, p. 332.

16. Ibid.

17. Caroli, p. 133.

18. Colman, p. 335.

19. Caroli, p. 134.

20. Ibid, p. 132.

ELLEN AXSON WILSON

1. Smith, N. and Ryan, M. (1989) *Modern First Ladies: Their Documentary Legacy.* Washington, D.C: National Archives and Records Administration, p. 32.

2. Ibid.

3. Caroli, B. (2010) *First Ladies: From Martha Washington to Michelle Obama.* 4th ed. New York: Oxford University Press, p. 138.

4. Miller Center, (n.d.) *Ellen Wilson.* [online] Available at: https://millercenter.org/president/wilson/essays/wilson-ellen-1913-firstlady [Accessed 31 Oct. 2019].

5. National First Ladies' Library, (n.d.). *First Lady Biography: Ellen Wilson.* [online] Available at: http://www.firstladies.org/biographies/firstladies.aspx?biography=28 [Accessed 31 Oct. 2019].

6. Wertheimer, M. (2004) *Inventing a Voice: The Rhetoric of American First Ladies of the Twentieth Century.* Lanham: Rowman & Littlefield Publishers, Inc., p. 83.

7. Smith.

8. Miller Center.

9. Swain, S. (2016) *First Ladies: Presidential Historians on the Lives of 45 Iconic American Women.* New York: PublicAffairs, p. 241.

10. Wertheimer, p. 90.

11. Ibid.

12. Bicknell, E. (1914) 'The Home-Maker of the White House: Mrs. Woodrow Wilson's Social Work in Washington', *The Survey,* (33), p. 22.

EDITH BOLLING GALT WILSON

1. Colman, E. (1927) *White House Gossip: from Andrew Johnson to Calvin Coolidge,* Garden City: Doubleday, Page & Company, p. 358.

2. Swain, S. (2016) *First Ladies: Presidential Historians on the Lives of 45 Iconic American Women.* New York: PublicAffairs, p. 246.

3. Wertheimer, p. 117.

4. Wilson, E. (1980) *My memoir.* New York: Arno Press, p. 284.

5. Colman, p. 374.

6. Ibid.

7. Ibid, p. 289.

8. Ibid.

9. Cooper, J. (2001) *Breaking the Heart of the World: Woodrow Wilson and the Fight for the League of Nations.* Cambridge: Cambridge University Press, p. 202.

10. Ibid.

11. Ibid.

12. Wilson, p. 289.

13. Ibid.

14. Colman, p. 367.

15. Ibid, p. 366.

16. Wertheimer, M. (2004) *Inventing a Voice: The Rhetoric of American First Ladies of the Twentieth Century.* Lanham: Rowman & Littlefield Publishers, Inc., p. 110.

17. Colman, p. 366.

FLORENCE KING HARDING

1. Caroli, B. (2010) *First Ladies: From Martha Washington to Michelle Obama.* 4th ed. New York: Oxford University Press, p. 160.

2. Ibid.

3. National First Ladies' Library. (n.d.) *First Lady Biography: Florence Harding.* [online] Available at: http://www.firstladies.org/biographies/firstladies.aspx?biography=30 [Accessed 3 Nov. 2019].

4. Caroli, p. 161.

5. Ibid, p. 162.

6. Anthony, C. (1988) 'Mediums and Messages', *The Washington Post* [online]. Available at: https://www.washingtonpost.com/archive/lifestyle/1988/05/04/mediums-and-messages/e28b3463-2c78-4ab6-8cca-9382357fd018/ [Accessed 3 Nov. 2019].

7. Ibid.

8. Ibid.

9. Dean, J. (2004) *Warren G. Harding,* New York: Times Books, p. 56.

10. Ibid.

11. Ibid.

12. Caroli, p. 165.

13. Baker, P. (2015) 'DNA Shows Warren Harding Wasn't America's First Black President', *The Washington Post* [online]. Available at: https://www.nytimes.com/2015/08/19/us/politics/dna-that-confirmed-one-warren-harding-rumor-refutes-another.html [Accessed 3 Nov. 2019].

14. Caroli, p. 165.

15. Whitcomb, J. and Whitcomb, C. (2002) *Real Life at the White House: Two Hundred Years of Daily Life at America's Most Famous Residence.* New York: Routledge, p. 263.

16. Beasley, M. (2005) *First Ladies and the Press: The Unfinished Partnership of the Media Age.* Evanston: Northwestern University Press, p. 53.

17. Ibid, p. 54.

18. Ibid.

19. Caroli, p. 166.

20. Glass, A. (2017) *President Harding dies in San Francisco, Aug. 2, 1923.* [online] Available at: https://www.politico.com/story/2017/08/02/president-harding-dies-in-san-francisco-aug-2-1923-241148

[Accessed 3 Nov. 2019].

GRACE ANNA GOODHUE COOLIDGE

1. Caroli, B. (2010) *First Ladies: From Martha Washington to Michelle Obama*. 4th ed. New York: Oxford University Press, p. 158.
2. Beasley, M. (2005) *First Ladies and the Press: The Unfinished Partnership of the Media Age*. Evanston: Northwestern University Press, p. 55.
3. Burns, P. (1926) 'The First Lady', The New Yorker, (15 May issue), p. 17.
4. Ibid.
5. Ibid.
6. Ibid.
7. Coolidge, G. (1992) *Grace Coolidge: An Autobiography*. Worland: High Plains Publishing Company, p. 62.
8. Caroli, p. 174.
9. Ibid.
10. Calvin Coolidge Presidential Foundation. (n.d.) *Grace Coolidge Overview*. [online] Available at: https://www.coolidgefoundation.org/presidency/grace-coolidge-overview/ [Accessed 6 Nov. 2019].
11. Ibid.
12. Beasley, p. 55.

LOU HENRY HOOVER

1. National First Ladies' Library. (n.d.) First Lady Biography: Lou Hoover. [online]. Available at: http://www.firstladies.org/biographies/firstladies.aspx?biography=32 [Accessed 8 Nov. 2019].
2. Swain, S. (2016) *First Ladies: Presidential Historians on the Lives of 45 Iconic American Women*. New York: PublicAffairs, p. 278.
3. Ibid.
4. Miller Center. (n.d.) *Lou Hoover* [online]. Available at: https://millercenter.org/president/hoover/essays/hoover-1929-firstlady [Accessed 8 Nov. 2019].
5. Slach, J. (2015) *Lou Hoover's Reflections on Reflectors* [online]. Available at: https://hoover.blogs.archives.gov/2015/12/03/lou-hoovers-reflections-on-reflectors/ [Accessed 8 Nov. 2019].
6. Ross, I. (1936) *Ladies of the Press*. 5th ed. New York: Harper & Brothers, p. 314.
7. Ibid.
8. Parry-Giles, S. and Blair, D. (2002) 'The Rise of the Rhetorical First Lady: Politics, Gender Ideology, and Women's Voice', *Rhetoric & Public Affairs* 5(4), p. 528 [online]. Available at: https://www.jstor.org/stable/41940289 [Accessed 8 Nov. 2019].

ANNA ELEANOR ROOSEVELT

1. Caroli, B. (2010) *First Ladies: From Martha Washington to Michelle Obama*. 4th ed. New York: Oxford University Press, p. 191.
2. Black, A. (1996) *Casting Her Own Shadow: Eleanor Roosevelt and the Shaping of Postwar Liberalism*. New York: Columbia University Press, p. 7.
3. Ibid.
4. Ibid, p. 8.
5. Breitzer, S. (2006) 'Eleanor Roosevelt: An Unlikely Path to Political Activist', in Watson R. and Eksterowicz A., (eds.), *The Presidential Companion: Readings on the First Ladies*, 2nd ed. Columbia: University of South Carolina Press, p. 154.
6. Breitzer, p. 155.
7. Ibid.
8. Fenster, J. (2009) *FDR's Shadow: Louis Howe, The Force That Shaped Franklin and Eleanor Roosevelt*. London: Palgrave Macmillan, p. 123.
9. Fenster, p. 222.
10. Clift, E. (2017) *Eleanor Roosevelt: Feminist Icon* [online]. Available at: https://www.thedailybeast.com/eleanor-roosevelt-feminist-icon [Accessed 13

Nov. 2019].
11. Ibid.
12. Roosevelt, E. (1928) 'Women Must Learn to Play the Game as Men Do', *Red Book Magazine*, Volume 50, pp. 141–42 [online]. Available at: https://www2.gwu.edu/~erpapers/documents/articles/womenmustlearn.cfm [Accessed 13 Nov. 2019].
13. Ibid.
14. Roosevelt, E. (1949) *This I Remember*. New York: Harper & Brothers, p. 74.
15. Ibid.
16. Breitzer, p. 150.
17. Beasley, M. (1986) 'Eleanor Roosevelt's Vision of Journalism: A Communications Medium for Women' *Presidential Studies Quarterly*, Volume 16(1), p. 67 [online]. Available at: https://www.jstor.org/stable/27550311 [Accessed 13 Nov. 2019].
18. Ibid.
19. The Eleanor Roosevelt Papers. (2006) *"My Day"* Column (1935–1962). [online] Available at: https://www2.gwu.edu/~erpapers/mep/displaydoc.cfm?docid=erpo-myday [Accessed 13 Nov. 2019].
20. Caroli, pp. 198–99.

ELIZABETH VIRGINIA WALLACE TRUMAN

1. Morris, S. (1986) 'Lady from Independence,' *The Washington Post* [online]. Available at: https://www.washingtonpost.com/archive/entertainment/books/1986/05/04/lady-from-independence/9ef3f8d7-972c-4339-af5a-2a7cbb307cb8/ [Accessed 17 Nov. 2019].
2. Wong, K. (2009) 'The Private Life of a Presidential Wife: Bess Truman Letters to Husband Harry Revealed to Public,' *ABC News* [online]. Available at: https://abcnews.go.com/Politics/lady-bess-trumans-letters-president-harry-truman-show/story?id=8831003 [Accessed 17 Nov. 2019].
3. Wertheimer, M. (2004). *Inventing a Voice: The Rhetoric of American First Ladies of the Twentieth Century*. Lanham: Rowman & Littlefield Publishers, Inc., p. 211.
4. Ibid.
5. Ibid.
6. Frey, R. (2006) 'Bess Truman: The Reluctant First Lady' in Watson R. and Eksterowicz A. (eds.), *The Presidential Companion: Readings on the First Ladies*, 2nd ed. Columbia: University of South Carolina Press, p. 126.
7. Van der Heuvel, G. (1982) 'Remembering Bess', *The Washington Post* [online]. Available at: https://www.washingtonpost.com/archive/lifestyle/1982/10/19/remembering-bess/3ad55764-5296-4dd5-8ef1-8b2464067456/ [Accessed 17 Nov. 2019].
8. Ibid.
9. Caroli, B. (2010) *First Ladies: From Martha Washington to Michelle Obama*. 4th ed. New York: Oxford University Press, p. 206.
10. Beasley, M. (2005) *First Ladies and the Press: The Unfinished Partnership of the Media Age*. Evanston: Northwestern University Press, p. 62.
11. Truman, M. (1986) *Bess W. Truman*. New York: Macmillan, p. 279.
12. Truman, pp. 278–79.
13. Powell, A. (1971) *Adam by Adam: The Autobiography of Adam Clayton Powell, Jr.* New York: Kensington Publishing Corporation, p. 79.
14. Truman, p. 279.
15. Beasley, p. 65.

MAMIE GENEVA DOUD EISENHOWER

1. Henney, E. (1942) 'Presenting Mrs. Eisenhower', *The Washington Post* [online] by S3. Available at: https://search-proquest-com.i.ezproxy.nypl.org/hnpwashingtonpost/docview/151521263/

B640DAD40F7D44A2PQ/ [Accessed 20 Nov. 2019].
2. Ibid.
3. Ibid.
4. Ibid.
5. Beasley, M. (2005) *First Ladies and the Press: The Unfinished Partnership of the Media Age*. Evanston: Northwestern University Press, p. 66.
6. Teasley, M. (1987) 'Ike Was Her Career: The Papers of Mamie Doud Eisenhower', *The Journal of the National Archives*, 19(1), p. 112.
7. Ibid.
8. Ibid.
9. Troy, G. (2006) 'Copresident or Codependent? The Rise and Rejection of Presidential Couples since World War II', in Watson R. and Eksterowicz A. (eds.) *The Presidential Companion: Readings on the First Ladies*, 2nd ed. Columbia: University of South Carolina Press, p. 258.
10. Ibid.
11. Teasley, p. 109.
12. Ibid.
13. Troy, p. 257.
14. Teasley, p. 112.
15. Ibid.
16. Troy, p. 257.
17. Teasley, p. 114.

JACQUELINE LEE BOUVIER KENNEDY

1. Beasley, M. (2005) *First Ladies and the Press: The Unfinished Partnership of the Media Age*. Evanston: Northwestern University Press, p. 72.
2. Ibid.
3. Ibid, pp. 72–73.
4. Ibid, p. 79.
5. Nilsson, J. (2014) 'Falling for Jackie Kennedy', *The Saturday Evening Post* [online]. Available at: https://www.saturdayeveningpost.com/2014/04/falling-for-jackie-kennedy/ [Accessed 21 Nov. 2019].
6. Ibid.
7. Troy, G. (2001) 'Jacqueline Kennedy's White House Renovations', *White House Studies*, Volume 1(3) [online]. Available at: https://go.gale.com/psido?v=2.1&it=r&sw=w&id=-GALE%7CA82476772&prodId=AON-E&sid=googleScholarFullText&userGroupName=new55117 [Accessed 21 Nov. 2019].
8. Ibid.
9. Ibid.
10. Moe, R. and Zax, L. (1994) 'Jackie's Washington: How She Rescued The City's History', *The Washington Post* [online]. Available at: https://www.washingtonpost.com/archive/opinions/1994/05/29/jackies-washington-how-she-rescued-the-citys-history/5d59d26d-659d-451d-8303-e2f19c4a7175/ [Accessed 21 Nov. 2019].
11. Ibid.
12. Troy.
13. Ibid.
14. Johnson, L. (2001) 'Selections from Lady Bird's Diary on the assassination', *PBS* [online]. Available at: https://www.pbs.org/ladybird/epicenter/epicenter_doc_diary.html [Accessed 21 Nov. 2019].
15. Piereson, J. (2013) *How Jackie Kennedy Invented the Camelot Legend After JFK's Death*. [online] Available at: https://www.thedailybeast.com/how-jackie-kennedy-invented-the-camelot-legend-after-jfks-death [Accessed 21 Nov. 2019].
16. Ibid.
17. Sooke, A. (2014) 'Jackie Kennedy: Andy Warhol's pop saint', *BBC Culture* [online]. https://www.bbc.com/culture/article/20140418-jackie-warhols-pop-saint [Accessed 21 Nov. 2019].

CLAUDIA TAYLOR "LADY BIRD" JOHNSON

1. Beasley, M. (2005) *First Ladies and the Press: The Unfinished Partnership of the Media Age.* Evanston: Northwestern University Press, p. 90.

2. Ibid, p. 91.

3. Florio, G. (2007) 'Former first lady Lady Bird Johnson dies', *The Philadelphia Inquirer* [online]. Available at: https://www.inquirer.com/philly/news/breaking/20070711_Former_first_lady_Lady_Bird_Johnson_dies.html [Accessed 2 Dec. 2019].

4. Ibid.

5. Marton, K. (2001) *Hidden Power: Presidential Marriages That Shaped Our History.* New York: Anchor Books, p. 145.

6. Ibid.

7. Beasley, p. 93.

8. Ibid.

9. National Park Service. (n.d.) *Beautification: A Legacy of Lady Bird Johnson* [online]. Available at: https://www.nps.gov/articles/lady-bird-johnson-beautification-cultural-landscapes.htm [Accessed 2 Dec. 2019].

10. Beasley, p. 96.

11. Ibid.

12. Kelly, J. (2015) 'Springtime in Washington wouldn't be the same without Lady Bird Johnson', *The Washington Post* [online]. Available at: https://www.washingtonpost.com/local/springtime-in-washington-wouldnt-be-the-same-without-lady-bird-johnson/2015/03/18/36ea99c2-ccc5-11e4-8a46-b1dc9be5a8ff_story.html [Accessed 2 Dec. 2019].

13. Black, A. (2009) *Claudia Alta Taylor 'Lady Bird' Johnson* [online]. Available at: https://www.whitehouse.gov/about-the-white-house/first-ladies/claudia-alta-taylor-lady-bird-johnson/ [Accessed 2 Dec. 2019].

PATRICIA RYAN NIXON

1. Lewine, F. (1974) 'Politics: A life she would not have chosen', *The Associated Press* (printed in The Daily Register), p. 8.

2. Ibid.

3. Mazo, E. (1959) *Richard Nixon: a Political and Personal Portrait.* New York: Harper & Brothers, pp. 41–45.

4. Ibid.

5. Swain, S. (2016) *First Ladies: Presidential Historians on the Lives of 45 Iconic American Women.* New York: PublicAffairs, p. 358.

6. Bostock. B. (2019) *Patricia Nixon's Visitor Friendly White House* [online]. Available at: https://www.whitehousehistory.org/patricia-nixons-visitor-friendly-white-house [Accessed 3 Dec. 2019].

7. Lewine.

8. Christensen, D. (1986) 'Real America Bowls Them Over', *Los Angeles Times* [online]. Available at: https://www.latimes.com/archives/la-xpm-1986-09-30-mn-10250-story.html [Accessed 4 Dec. 2019].

9. Anon. (1993) 'Pat Nixon Dies; Model Political Wife Was 81', *Los Angeles Times* [online]. Available at: https://www.latimes.com/archives/la-xpm-1993-06-23-mn-6290-story.html [Accessed 4 Dec. 2019].

ELIZABETH BLOOMER FORD

1. McCubbin, L. (2018) *Betty Ford: First Lady, Women's Advocate, Survivor, Trailblazer.* New York: Gallery Books, p. 151.

2. Ibid, p. 45.

3. Gallup. (n.d.) *Most Admired Man and Woman* [online]. Available at: https://news.gallup.com/poll/1678/most-admired-man-woman.aspx [Accessed 6 Dec. 2019].

4. Watson R. and Eksterowicz A. (eds) (2006) The *Presidential Companion: Readings on the First Ladies,* 2nd ed. Columbia: University of South Carolina Press, p. 291.

5. Anon. (1987). 'New Attitudes Ushered In by Betty Ford', *The New York Times* [online]. Available at: https://www.nytimes.com/1987/10/17/us/new-attitudes-ushered-in-by-betty-ford.html

6. Tobin, L. (1990) 'Eleanor Roosevelt's Vision of Journalism: A Communications Medium for Women', *Presidential Studies Quarterly,* Volume 20(4), p. 763 [online]. Available at: https://www.jstor.org/stable/20700159 [Accessed 6 Dec. 2019].

7. Nichols, J. (2011) 'Betty Ford: Feminist, Social Liberal, Republican', *The Nation* [online]. Available at: https://www.thenation.com/article/betty-ford-feminist-social-liberal-republican/ [Accessed 6 Dec. 2019].

8. Anon. (1975) 'Betty Ford Would Accept "An Affair" By Daughter', *The New York Times* [online]. Available at: https://www.nytimes.com/1975/08/11/archives/betty-ford-would-accept-art-affair-by-daughter.html [Accessed 6 Dec. 2019].

9. Tobin, p. 761.

10. Nichols.

ROSALYNN SMITH CARTER

1. Hunter, M. (1978) 'Mrs. Carter at Work in Presidential Partnership', *The New York Times* [online]. Available at: https://www.nytimes.com/1978/02/14/archives/mrs-carter-at-work-in-presidential-partnership-mental-health-is-one.html [Accessed 13 Dec. 2019].

2. Ayres Jr., B. (1976) 'The Importance of Being Rosalynn', *The New York Times* [online]. Available at: https://www.nytimes.com/1979/06/03/archives/the-importance-of-being-rosalynn-first-lady-on-the-move.html [Accessed 13 Dec. 2019].

3. Watson R. and Eksterowicz A. (eds) (2006) The *Presidential Companion: Readings on the First Ladies,* 2nd ed. Columbia: University of South Carolina Press, p. 221.

4. Ayres.

5. Wertheimer, M. (2004) *Inventing a Voice: The Rhetoric of American First Ladies of the Twentieth Century.* Lanham: Rowman & Littlefield Publishers, Inc., p. 346.

6. Beasley, M. (2005) *First Ladies and the Press: The Unfinished Partnership of the Media Age.* Evanston: Northwestern University Press, p. 149.

7. Ibid, p. 154.

8. Radcliffe, D. (1980) 'Tears & Pride of The Steel Magnolia: Rosalynn Carter on the Aftermath', *The Washington Post* [online]. Available at: https://www.washingtonpost.com/archive/lifestyle/1980/11/19/tears-38/6becb957-8fe8-4adf-b5d4-800489012ce3/ [Accessed 13 Dec. 2019].

NANCY DAVIS REAGAN

1. Cannon, L. (2016) 'Nancy Reagan, an Influential and Protective First Lady, Dies at 94', *The New York Times* [online]. Available at: https://www.nytimes.com/2016/03/07/us/nancy-reagan-a-stylish-and-influential-first-lady-dies-at-94.html [Accessed 14 Dec. 2019].

2. Ibid.

3. Warner, M. (2016) 'Nancy Reagan, her husband's true 'Iron Lady'', *PBS NewsHour* [online]. Available at: https://www.pbs.org/newshour/politics/nancy-reagan-her-husbands-true-iron-lady [Accessed 14 Dec. 2019].

4. Purdum, T. (2014). *The vanished Washington of Strauss* [online]. Available at: https://www.politico.

com/story/2014/03/the-vanished-washington-of-robert-strauss-104855 [Accessed 14 Dec. 2019].

5. Safire, W. (1987). 'The First Lady Stages a Coup', *The New York Times* [online]. Available at: https://www.nytimes.com/1987/03/02/opinion/essay-the-first-lady-stages-a-coup.html [Accessed 14 Dec. 2019].

6. Warner.

7. Reagan, N. (1989). *My Turn.* Random House: New York. pp. 46–47.

8. Harper, M. (2016) 'Former First Lady Nancy Reagan was known for her lavish style -- and Reagan red', *Los Angeles Times* [online]. Available at: https://www.latimes.com/fashion/la-ig-nancy-reagan-lavish-style-reagan-red-20160306-story.html [Accessed 14 Dec. 2019].

9. Reagan, p. 35.

10. Ibid. p. 36.

BARBARA PIERCE BUSH

1. Carlson, M. (1989) 'The Silver Fox', *Time* [online]. Available at: http://content.time.com/time/magazine/article/0,9171,956782,00.html [Accessed 17 Dec. 2019].

2. Radcliffe, D. (1989) 'Barbara Bush, being herself', *The Washington Post* [online]. Available at: https://www.washingtonpost.com/archive/lifestyle/1989/01/15/barbara-bush-being-herself/2cfe5c47-559b-4647-a77f-2a48303cda32/ [Accessed 17 Dec. 2019].

3. Troy, G. (2006) 'Copresident or Codependent? The Rise and Rejection of Presidential Couples since World War II' in Watson R. and Eksterowicz A. (eds.) *The Presidential Companion: Readings on the First Ladies,* 2nd ed. Columbia: University of South Carolina Press, p. 264.

4. Radcliffe.

5. Page, S. (2019) 'Barbara Bush's Long-Hidden 'Thoughts on Abortion'.' *The Atlantic* [online]. Available at: https://www.theatlantic.com/ideas/archive/2019/03/how-barbara-bush-decided-she-was-pro-choice/585589/ [Accessed 17 Dec. 2019].

6. Hunt, T. (2018) 'The day outspoken Barbara Bush regretted speaking her mind', *The Associated Press* [online]. Available at: https://apnews.com/23a9a93d2a5a456fbccf48c70ec140f2/The-day-outspoken-Barbara-Bush-regretted-speaking-her-mind [Accessed 17 Dec. 2019].

7. Ibid.

8. Bunting, G. (1992) 'Barbara Bush: the President's Biggest Asset in a Time of Political Trouble', *Los Angeles Times* [online]. Available at: https://www.latimes.com/archives/la-xpm-1992-05-31-op-1424-story.html [Accessed 17 Dec. 2019].

9. Nemy, E. (2018) 'Barbara Bush, Wife of 41st President and Mother of 43rd, Dies at 92', *The New York Times* [online]. Available at: https://www.nytimes.com/2018/04/17/us/barbara-bush-dead.html [Accessed 17 Dec. 2019].

10. Ibid.

HILLARY RODHAM CLINTON

1. Jacob, M. (2016) 'When the Chicago Tribune scolded a "girl" named Hillary Clinton', *Chicago Tribune* [online]. Available at: https://www.chicagotribune.com/news/ct-clinton-trump-tribune-archives-met-20160930-story.html [Accessed 18 Dec. 2019].

2. Ibid.

3. Ibid.

4. Ibid.

5. Gutin, M. (2006) 'Hillary's Choices' in Watson R. and Eksterowicz A. (eds.) *The Presidential Companion: Readings on the First Ladies,* 2nd ed. Columbia: University of South Carolina Press, p. 279.

6. Ibid.

7. Ibid.

8. Ingwerson, M. (1993) *Ruling That Hillary Clinton Isn't an "Official" Clouds Her Role* [online]. Available at: https://www.csmonitor.com/1993/0312/12011.html [Accessed 18 Dec. 2019].

9. Pear, R. (1993) 'Court Rules That First Lady Is "De Facto" Federal Official', *The New York Times* [online]. Available at: https://www.nytimes.com/1993/06/23/us/court-rules-that-first-lady-is-de-facto-federal-official.html [Accessed 18 Dec. 2019].

10. Fallows, J. (1995) 'A Triumph of Misinformation', *The Atlantic* [online]. Available at: https://www.theatlantic.com/magazine/archive/1995/01/a-triumph-of-misinformation/306231/ [Accessed 18 Dec. 2019].

11. Today. (1998) *NBC* [TV broadcast]

12. Gutin, p. 282.

LAURA WELCH BUSH

1. Kennedy, R. (2004) 'The First Lady; The Not-So-Reluctant Bush Campaigner' *The New York Times* [online]. Available at: https://www.nytimes.com/2004/08/12/us/the-2004-campaign-the-first-lady-the-not-so-reluctant-bush-campaigner.html [Accessed 20 Dec. 2019].

2. Ibid.

3. Allen, M. (2001) 'Laura Bush Gives Radio Address'. *The Washington Post* [online]. Available at: https://www.washingtonpost.com/archive/politics/2001/11/18/laura-bush-gives-radio-address/670a30a8-7c47-4669-a888-b88735fe68dc/ [Accessed 20 Dec. 2019].

4. Bumiller, E. (2002) 'Teach the Children Well, First Lady Urges Senators', *The New York Times* [online]. Available at: https://www.nytimes.com/2002/01/25/us/teach-the-children-well-first-lady-urges-senators.html [Accessed 20 Dec. 2019].

5. Ibid.

6. Turner, C. (2015) 'No Child Left Behind: What Worked, What Didn't', *NPR* [online]. Available at: https://www.npr.org/sections/ed/2015/10/27/443110755/no-child-left-behind-what-worked-what-didnt [Accessed 22 Dec. 2019].

7. Kennedy.

8. Ibid.

9. Jones, J. (2006) *Laura Bush Approval Ratings Among Best for First Ladies* [online]. Available at: https://news.gallup.com/poll/21370/laura-bush-approval-ratings-among-best-first-ladies.aspx [Accessed 20 Dec. 2019].

10. Gallup, (n.d.) *Presidential Approval Ratings – George W. Bush* [online]. Available at: https://news.gallup.com/poll/116500/presidential-approval-ratings-george-bush.aspx [Accessed 22 Dec. 2019].

11. Ibid.

12. Doyle, S. (2010) 'The Secret Inner Life of Laura Bush', *The Atlantic* [online]. Available at: https://www.theatlantic.com/entertainment/archive/2010/05/the-secret-inner-life-of-laura-bush/56644/ [Accessed 20 Dec. 2019].

13. Goldman, R. (2010) 'Laura Bush Reveals How George W. Bush Stopped Drinking', *ABC News* [online]. Available at: https://abcnews.go.com/Politics/laura-bush-reveals-george-stopped-drinking/story?id=10552148 [Accessed 20 Dec. 2019].

MICHELLE OBAMA

1. NPR. (2012) *Transcript: Michelle Obama's Convention Speech* [online]. Available at: https://www.npr.org/2012/09/04/160578836/transcript-michelle-obamas-convention-speech Accessed 28 Dec. 2019].

2. Obama, M. (2018) *Becoming.* Crown: New York,

p. 71.

3. Ibid, p. 80.

4. Silva, D. (2017) 'Michelle Obama: The Historic Legacy of the Nation's First Black First Lady', *NBC News* [online]. Available at: https://www.nbcnews.com/storyline/president-obama-the-legacy/michelle-obama-historic-legacy-nation-s-first-black-first-lady-n703506 [Accessed 26 Dec. 2019].

5. Saulny, S. (2008) 'Michelle Obama Thrives in Campaign Trenches', *The New York Times* [online]. Available at: https://www.nytimes.com/2008/02/14/us/politics/14michelle.html [Accessed 26 Dec. 2019].

6. Ibid.

7. Ibid.

8. Kantor, J. (2009) 'Michelle Obama Goes Sleeveless, Again', *The New York Times* [online]. Available at: https://thecaucus.blogs.nytimes.com/2009/02/25/michelle-obama-goes-sleeveless-again/ [Accessed 26 Dec. 2019].

9. Silva.

10. Taylor, D. (2017) 'More than 'mom-in-chief': Michelle Obama bows out as dynamic first lady', *The Guardian* [online]. Available at: https://www.theguardian.com/us-news/2017/jan/06/michelle-obama-legacy-first-lady [Accessed 26 Dec. 2019].

MELANIA TRUMP

1. Horowitz, J. (2016) 'Melania Trump: From Small-Town Slovenia to Doorstep of White House', *The New York Times* [online]. Available at: https://www.nytimes.com/2016/07/19/us/politics/melania-trump-slovenia.html [Accessed 28 Dec. 2019].

2. Ibid.

3. Collins, L. (2016) 'The Model American', *The New Yorker* [online]. Available at: https://www.newyorker.com/magazine/2016/05/09/who-is-melania-trump [Accessed 28 Dec. 2019].

4. Kuczynski, A. (2016) 'Melania Trump's American Dream', *Harper's Bazaar* [online]. Available at: https://www.harpersbazaar.com/culture/features/a13529/melania-trump-interview-0216/ [Accessed 28 Dec. 2019].

5. Ibid.

6. Jaffe, A. (2016) 'Melania Trump Republican Convention Speech Bears Striking Similarities to Michelle Obama Address', *NBC News* [online]. Available at: https://www.nbcnews.com/politics/2016-election/melania-trump-appears-plagiarize-michelle-obama-convention-speech-n612141 [Accessed 28 Dec. 2019].

7. Collins.

8. Belam, M. (2018) '"Missing" Melania Trump breaks silence after 20-day absence', *The Guardian* [online]. Available at: https://www.theguardian.com/us-news/2018/may/31/missing-melania-trump-breaks-silence-absence-tweet [Accessed 30 Dec. 2019].

9. Heil, E. (2019) 'Melania Trump's office cut in half and White House residence has skeleton crew during shutdown', *The Washington Post* [online]. Available at: https://www.washingtonpost.com/lifestyle/style/melania-trumps-office-cut-in-half-and-white-house-residence-has-skeleton-crew-during-shutdown/2019/01/15/b6beca58-1918-11e9-8813-cb9dec761e73_story.html [Accessed 30 Dec. 2019].

10. Trump, D. (2019) *So ridiculous. Greta must work on her Anger Management problem, then go to a good old fashioned movie with a friend! Chill Greta, Chill!* Twitter [online]. Available at: https://twitter.com/realdonaldtrump/status/1205100602025545730 [Accessed 30 Dec. 2019].

11. Puente, M. (2019) 'Melania Trump responds

to POTUS attack on Greta Thunberg; she says she 'communicates differently'', *USA Today* [online]. Available at: https://www.usatoday.com/story/entertainment/celebrities/2019/12/13/melania-trump-responds-potus-attack-thunberg/2640897001/ [Accessed 30 Dec. 2019].

12. Russo, A. (2019) 'Melania Trump Calls Journalists 'Opportunists' Piggybacking On Husband's Fame', *HuffPost* [online]. Available at: https://www.huffpost.com/entry/melania-trump_n_5c125fe6e-4b002a46c14c4db [Accessed 30 Dec. 2019].

13. Bennett, K. (2019) '"Free, Melania" offers new details about the life of a private first lady', *CNN* [online]. Available at: https://www.cnn.com/2019/12/02/politics/melania-trump-white-house-biography-free-melania/index.html [Accessed 28 Dec. 2019].

14. Kuczynski.

15. Ibid.

JILL BIDEN

1. Lozada, C. (2015) 'From 'Jill' to 'Mom' — inside Jill Biden's relationship with Beau and Hunter', *The Washington Post* [online]. Available at: https://www.washingtonpost.com/news/book-party/wp/2015/06/04/from-jill-to-mom-inside-jill-bidens-relationship-with-beau-and-hunter/ [Accessed 7 Nov. 2020]

2. Westfall, S. (2009) 'Jill Biden 'I Can Have It All'', *People* [online]. Available at: https://people.com/archive/jill-biden-i-can-have-it-all-vol-71-no-8/ [Accessed 7 Nov. 2020]

3. Biden, J. (2010) *Shining a Light on a Best Kept Secret* [online]. Available at: https://obamawhitehouse.archives.gov/blog/2010/10/07/shining-a-light-a-best-kept-secret [Accessed 6 Nov. 2020]

4. Schultz, C. (2019) 'Jill Biden's memoir — like Michelle Obama's — is not meant to be political', *The Washington Post* [online]. Available at: https://www.washingtonpost.com/outlook/jill-bidens-memoir--like-michelle-obamas--is-not-meant-to-be-political/2019/05/08/90016350-6e66-11e9-8f44-e8d8bb1df986_story.html [Accessed 8 Nov. 2020]

5. Glueck, K. and Corasaniti, N. (2020) 'Jill Biden, in D.N.C. Speech, Highlights Pandemic Concerns Among Teachers and Parents', *The New York Times* [online]. Available at: https://www.nytimes.com/2020/08/18/us/politics/jill-biden-dnc-speech.html [Accessed 8 Nov. 2020]

6. Yuan, J. and Linskey, A. (2020) 'Jill Biden is finally ready to be first lady. Can she help her husband beat Trump?', *The Washington Post* [online]. Available at: https://www.washingtonpost.com/lifestyle/style/jill-biden-is-finally-ready-to-be-first-lady-can-she-help-her-husband-beat-trump/2020/08/17/acacc936-e007-11ea-8181-606e603bb1c4_story.html [Accessed 7 Nov. 2020]

7. Ibid.

8. BBC, (2020) *Jill Biden: From teacher to US first lady* [online]. Available at: https://www.bbc.com/news/election-us-2020-53833061 [Accessed 6 Nov. 2020]

9. CBS Sunday Morning. (2020) *Dr. Jill Biden on family, teaching, loss and levity* [video] Available at: https://www.youtube.com/watch?v=DOYs_F5L-0Bc [Accessed 7 Nov. 2020]

CREDITS

The publishers would like to thank the following sources for their kind permission to reproduce the pictures in this book.

Alamy: Everett Collection Historical 35; /The Granger Collection 23, 27, 61; /Pictures Now 25; /Science History Images 33, 37, 57

Bridgeman Images: 13, 15; /Photo © Christie's Images 18

Cornell University Library: 93

Getty Images: Jean-Louis Atlan/Sygma 163; /Robyn Beck/ AFP 167; /Charles M Bell/PhotoQuest 99; /Bettmann 22, 51, 109, 115, 149, 154-155; /Brady-Handy/Epics 81; /Ed Clark/ The LIFE Picture Collection 136, 137, 140; /Corbis 125, 132-133, 162; /Education Images/Universal Images Group 44; / Granger 74; / Dirck Halstead/The LIFE Images Collection 150, 157; /Horst P. Horst/Conde Nast 153; /David Hume Kennerly 151; /Krisanne Johnson 171; /Saul Loeb/AFP 178; /Library of Congress 49, 85, 88, 119, 121; /Jeffrey Markowitz/Sygma 165; / Wally McNamee/CORBIS 147, 161; /Jeff J Mitchell 174; /MPI 17, 52-53, 70, 77; /PhotoQuest 101, 123, 131, 135; /Ronald Reagan Presidential Library 158; /George Silk/The LIFE Picture Collection 139; /Underwood And Underwood/The LIFE Images Collection 122; /Stan Wayman/The LIFE Picture Collection 145; /Universal History Archive 117; /Diana Walker//The LIFE Images Collection 159; /Jim Watson/AFP 181; /Oscar White/ Corbis/VCG 100; /The White House 177

Library of Congress: 10, 19, 26, 31, 34, 39, 41, 55, 59, 62, 63, 65, 66, 67, 71, 73, 82, 83, 87, 89, 91, 95, 96-97, 103, 104-105, 106, 111, 112, 113, 116, 128

Public Domain: 9, 29, 43, 47, 143

Franklin D. Roosevelt Presidential Library and Museum: NARA 126

Shutterstock: 175; /Granger 69, 79; /Kamran Jebreili/AP 170; / Photo Spirit 7

White House: 92, 169; /Joyce N. Boghosian/The White House 173

Every effort has been made to acknowledge correctly and contact the source and/or copyright holder of each picture and Welbeck Publishing apologises for any unintentional errors or omissions, which will be corrected in future editions of this book.